The
Jump
Rope
Book

The Jump Rope Book

by Elizabeth Loredo
Photographs by Martha Cooper

Workman Publishing
New York

Library of Congress Cataloging-in-Publication Data
Loredo, Elizabeth.
    The jump rope book/by Elizabeth Loredo: Photographs by
Martha Cooper.
    P. m.
    Includes indexes.
Summary: Describes the history, techniques, and variations of
jump rope games, with all kinds of rhymes used for skipping
rope.
ISBN 0-7611-0448-8
1. Rope skipping—juvenile literature. 2. Jump rope rhymes—
juvenile literature. (1. Rope skipping. 2. Jump rope rhymes.)
I. Cooper, Martha, ill. II. Title.
GV498.L67 1996   96-471
796.2—dc20   CIP
                                                        AC

Workman books are available at special discounts when
purchased in bulk for premiums and sales promotions as
well as for fundraising or educational use. Special editions
can also be created to specification. For details, contact the
special sales director at the address below.

Workman Publishing Company, Inc.
708 Broadway, New York, NY 10003-9555

Manufactured in the United States of America
First printing April 1996

10 9 8 7 6 5 4

Table of Contents

CHAPTER 3

CHAPTER 4

CHAPTER 5

CHAPTER 6

CHAPTER 7

CHAPTER 8

Two in the Middle:

CHAPTER 9

CHAPTER 10

Introduction

Jump rope has been around for thousands of years and will probably be around for thousands more. Why? Because it's the perfect game!

It's easy, cheap and fun. You can play with two, four, five players—or as big a group as you like. Then again, it's just as good with just one jumper. There are dozens of rhymes and games to play. It's even fun when you mess up. Now, how many games can claim all that?

One of the great things about jumping (some people say "skipping") rope is that there are so many ways to be good at it, and yet there's always some new triumph to shoot for. If you can jump thirty times in a row without missing, then you've created a new record just waiting to be broken—by you. If you're not so good at the running step, you may be able to skip a double bounce faster than anybody else. Maybe you know more rhymes than your friends or the one that always makes everyone laugh. Or perhaps you can turn a pepper that's faster than a whirling dervish.

Some rhymes make you laugh.

Jumping rope is all about fun. Bungling isn't an issue, since you always get a shot at jumping again. So it's not really about whether you win or lose but how you skip the rope.

Or how you turn it. For enders (some people say "turners"), the challenge is to work together to make the rope turn smoothy;

for jumpers, the goal is to go as long as possible without a miss. But even a miss is good in this game. It gives someone else a chance to play and allows the jumper time to rest up for another turn.

And then there are the rhymes. Everybody has a favorite. There are hundreds of them, from "Teddy Bear, Teddy Bear" to "Strawberry Shortcake," to "Dirty Bill from Vinegar Hill". With so many verses, there's something for everyone. Jump rope rhymes are special because they're passed along from kid to kid. Even this book worked that way— loads of rhymes were

Even if you're jumping on your own, it can be a challenge.

collected from kids who began by saying, "My sister told me this one" or "I got this from my best friend."

Rhymes are a great way to introduce yourself into the local playground group. Everyone wants to learn a new rhyme.

Many skipping rhymes are old and haven't altered much since your grandfather's mother was skipping to them. But they do change a bit, just as the kids who skip rope do, from generation to generation.

Jumping rope can be fun for a crowd...

Lots of rhymes are silly, because kids substitute new words that sound good for old ones they've forgotten. It's like an endless game of Telephone, with one kid telling another who tells another who tells another. It goes on forever. Something special in

...or a great game for one.

the rhythm and words make rhymes stick around and even travel the world. Hopefully, the same thing will happen with the rhymes in this book as they're passed from reader to friend.

So turn the pages and start skipping.

CHAPTER 1

A Jump Rope Scrap Book

How Old Is It?

Everyone agrees that jump rope is one of the world's oldest games, but no one knows exactly how long people have been skipping. Nobody's ever found an ancient jump rope—and probably no one ever will, because early skipping ropes were made of vines and twigs. Even the later ones made of cloth couldn't stand the test of time. The vines were thrown away at the end of the day; the cloth ropes rotted.

But we know they were there.

Early Games

The first games played by cave dwellers were undoubtedly contests to see who was strongest or fastest or who could jump higher. After all, these were the skills people needed just to survive. Anyone who could

In the days of the cave man, games were just ways to allow kids to grow strong and learn the ways of adults.

master them would win the admiration of others in the clan—and might avoid being a saber-tooth tiger's lunch.

It seems certain that some cave dwellers used a vine or flexible stick for jumping rope. Two Neanderthals might have held ends and pulled tight while a third leaped back and forth. Later, jump rope evolved when some enterprising cave dweller thought of swinging the vine while others jumped over it.

Way back then, and for a long time after, children's games were miniaturized, playful versions of adult pastimes. Children jumped and ran, imitating the fighting and hunting actions used by their parents. Jumping rope was good training for when they grew up, but they probably didn't care about that. It was just plain fun.

Ancient Egypt, Greece and Rome

While the Egyptians were wrapping mummies, their kids were skipping in the shadows of the pyramids. In ancient Greece and Rome, athletes were leaping hurdles, but their kids were having more fun jumping through hoops.

Things were hopping in China, too. A calendar from the sixth century shows that days were skipped away by Chinese kids during the Tang Dynasty.

Early skippers in England and Europe thought that jumping was not only fun but also somehow magical. It could predict the future and cast special charms. Jumpers today still use it to find the name of their future loves.

Some things never change.

Jump Rope's Dark Ages

The Middle Ages were tough on games and toys, but nothing could make kids stop skipping.

During the Dark Ages, religious leaders tried to destroy many of the customs of the day. But trick-or-treating, the midwinter giving of gifts, and skipping rope stuck around. They just became part of the new holidays of Halloween, Christmas and Easter.

At Easter time in England, people mobbed the streets in huge jump-roping crowds. Nobody is really sure why they choose skipping to celebrate Easter, but maybe any excuse was enough for a good game of jump rope. Some elements of wild fun lightened the Dark Ages, and jump rope was one of them.

Boys Have All the Fun

In Victorian times, young children—both boys and girls—were smothered in layers of thick underclothes, petticoats, and heavy dresses. The boys weren't imprisoned forever, though. They ditched the dresses when they got a little older and took

Victorian boys were allowed to ditch their heavy clothes when they got older.

to the street for games of marbles, hoops and, of course, jump rope.

Girls, however, were not so lucky. As they got older, more and more layers and gizmos were added to their

Victorian girls had to wear corsets like these under layers and layers of clothes.

costumes: undershirts, slips, petticoats, pinafores, bloomers, bodices, and heavy dresses. Under it all were stockings held up by garters, which would no doubt have fallen down with the slightest double-bounce.

The Victorians also had strange ideas about health. Girls were thought to be delicate and sickly. Girls were warned about the unhealthy effects of too much exercise. Even doctors of the time believed that girls could overstrain themselves with the slightest effort. They thought that skipping could cause a nervous breakdown!

But jump rope faced challenges even worse than odd ideas about

Poor children were used as cheap labor in factories during the 19th century.

exercise. Most little kids were kept too busy working to play games. Yes, working!

Children worked long hours in factories during Victorian times. But they still found time for games and jump rope was a favorite. Even poor kids could get their hands on a rope, and it was easy to carry one in a pocket for a game during breaks.

At this time Double Dutch jumping was introduced to American school-children by—you guessed it—the Dutch. It made its move across Europe and to the United States and soon had boys jumping double time on both sides of the ocean.

Girls were still left out of the loop, though. Most skipping was done by boys. They didn't chant rhymes but held contests to see who could make the most jumps.

Girls Take Over

Then, all at once, things got better, for kids and for skipping. The early 1900s were a great time for jump rope. America and Britain passed laws against child labor, and suddenly the streets were filled with children.

There weren't many playgrounds in those growing cities. Often, the sidewalk was the only safe place to play. So what better game for city boys than jump rope? It didn't take up much space, and a rope could be tucked away when a big crowd swarmed by. It was cheap—in fact you could make a jumprope from a length of your family's clothesline.

Skipping as a boy's game, played to win, was about to change.

◀ *In the 1900s, many girls began to jump rope.*

Girls started skipping in huge numbers, and their games were different from the boys'. The rhymes girls had chanted for other games had a wonderful beat for skipping. The whole idea behind jump rope changed almost overnight. It wasn't about winning a contest any more. It was about a group playing together, working as a team of enders and

Girls' jump rope games were more about cooperation than competition.

jumpers. It celebrated cooperation more than competition.

Girls went wild for the game. They kept finding and making up rhymes. More and more rhymes were added to the jumpers' lists.

But as the number of rhymes and games grew, fewer and fewer boys joined in. By taking the competitive edge away from skipping, the girls had won the game.

Jump rope stayed pretty much a girl's game for a long time. Boys could sometimes be caught in the ropes, but not often. It wasn't until the last twenty years, when skipping rope became connected to sporting competitions and training, that boys came back to jump rope.

Jumping for Health

Jumping rope is a lot more than just a game. Top athletes and high-tech sport doctors know that it prepares your body for quick-move sports like tennis, football and basketball. They incorporate a jump rope routine into training sessions. And just about every championship boxer uses a jump rope to build his stamina and enhance his lightning footwork.

If a jump rope work-out is a favorite of Heisman trophy winners, Wimbledon cup holders and heavyweight boxing champs—think what it can do for you.

Jim McCleary, 13, of Columbia, Maryland is the 1995 Junior Olympic Gold Medalist in the three jump rope events. He's been jumping since he was 3 years old. He is a member of the Kangaroo Kids precision jump rope team.

CHAPTER 2

Putting Your Best Foot Forward

Jumping Basics

You might think it's easy to jump rope. Ha! Think again. Were you able to keep your bike upright the first time you tried pedaling? Well, at first, jumping rope isn't easy either. Just like riding a bike it uses a complicated combination of foot and hand moves. Balancing and timing are tricky, too. And when you start getting into the really fancy footwork, look out. Those moves can make popping a wheelie look easy.

How to Jump

There's a reason it's called jump rope. You need a rope. You can use the one that comes with this book for jumping alone.

If you're jumping with more than one, you can raid your family clothesline or make a trip to any toy, sports or department store. You can buy jump ropes almost anywhere. The tricky part is getting one that's the right size for you and works best for the kind of jumping you want to do.

You'll need a rope to jump rope.

Jump Rope Fashions

High heels are a definite no-no! But bare feet aren't any better. Jumping rope is a high-impact sport, so wear athletic shoes.

The best footwear bets are sneakers and athletic shoes designed for aerobics and cross-training. They give you support under your toes and along the sides of your feet. That support could help prevent a twisted ankle.

Always wear socks, the cushier the better. Of course, if you go sockless, the rhymes about your feet stinking will have special meaning.

The foot fashion of jump rope is practical.

Your Mother Was Right

Well, she was. When she told you a hundred times to "stand up straight," she was preparing you to be a skipper. Good form helps you jump longer and improves your balance during the tougher moves. That doesn't mean you have to jump with a book on your head. But straighten that spine and try to keep your head up.

While jumping, tuck your elbows in close to your sides.

Bells and Whistles:
Decorating Your Rope

Jump ropes come in a rainbow of colors and materials. There are striped ones, plaid ones, see-through plastic ones, oh-so-serious professional rubber versions as well as the cheap fabric throw-away kind. How can you make yours stand out in that kind of crowd? Paint your rope, bead it, make it glitter and sparkle—even make it hairy!

There are many ways to make your rope unique.

There are dozens of stick-ons you can apply, from sequins, beads and charms, to googly eyes, jewels and wooden letters.

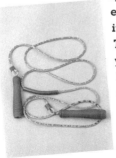

You can write messages or rhymes on your rope.

Hop to It

You've got the rope, the right shoes, and good form. Now it's time to put it all together.

Hold one handle in each hand. If your rope doesn't have handles, hold the ends firmly.

Start with the rope looped behind your back, just touching the backs of your ankles. Then begin to swing the rope behind you and over your head. Keep jumping until you get a comfortable, steady movement going. Gradually build

Wrap any slack around your hands so it doesn't dangle and get caught in the turning rope.

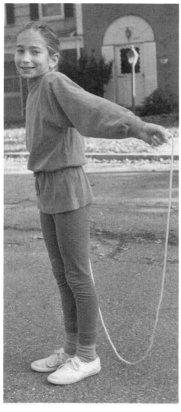

momentum. Don't use a big hop; jump lightly on your toes, just high enough for the rope to pass beneath. High jumps are hard on your knees and aren't quick enough.

The starting position for jumping rope is with the rope behind you.

Crowd Rules

There are other moves you'll need to master when jumping with other players. Running into a rope being turned by enders takes a lot of practice.

It takes practice to jump into the rope.

When first learning, choose friendly enders who have a lot of patience. You truly will be running right into the rope pretty often before you get the hang of the timing.

If you can't seem to get into the swing of things, don't give up! Keep practicing. Meanwhile, you can try a start-in-place jump. Stand beside the stopped rope, facing an ender. The enders begin by swinging the rope up and over your head and you start jumping from this standing position.

Sharing a rope can be tricky. When jumping with several skippers in the rope, be aware of where your elbows and knees are and where your feet are landing. Try not to trample. Two left feet can be a problem when there are four feet sharing the same space.

Pardon My Elbow

The current record for the most jumpers in synchronized jumping was made by kids attending the Yorkton Regional High School in Yorkton, located in Saskatchewan, Canada. In May of 1992, the students jumped the minimum of twelve turns needed for the record. You don't think twelve turns is all that much? See how many of your friends can jump together. Try it with just five friends, then ten. Not so easy, huh? Now imagine 260 kids jumping all at once. That's how many Yorkton students banded together to break the record for the most jumpers on one rope.

The record for most turns by a large group was won by students at the Ino Elementary school in Japan. Ninety jumpers managed 190 turns of the rope, with no breaks and no faults, before missing.

*How many jumpers can **you** fit in a rope?*

Jumping Options
One player

This one is fairly obvious. A "loner" jumps with one handle in each hand. Ropes for one are usually between 6 and 8 feet in length.

Loners can liven up their jumping by switching the direction of the rope's turn. Instead of swinging forward, swing the rope the opposite way, from front to back. Keep

A loner jumps by herself.

in mind that you'll be jumping "blind," sensing when the rope is about to reach the back of your feet.

Two players

Now you've got a few options. One jumper may skip while a friend turns an end; the other end of the rope is tied to a post or a handy doorknob.

Two can jump together: One

jumper stands close in behind the other. Each one takes an end, turning the rope over both jumpers. If coordinating the swings is a problem, one jumper may hold both ends.

Jumping with two in a rope takes concentration.

Two jumpers may try other skips, too. Each can take an end and jump side by side. More experienced twosomes can turn around into the spinning rope. Because the rope must be big enough to pass over both jumpers, it should be longer than the single-jumper rope, between 10 and 12 feet.

Three or more players

Two players each take an end of a long rope (the length depends on the number of jumpers). The two enders coordinate their turns so that the rope moves in a clean arc and doesn't wobble. The rope may be turned in either direction, and jumpers can enter from either side.

Basic Jumps

Here is a list of basic jumps to get you started. Follow the instructions and practice, practice, practice.

Double Bounce

Double Bounce This is a two-footed jump. You begin with a tiny, balancing hop as the rope comes up behind your head. Then there is a bigger jump as the rope passes under your feet.

Two-Foot Jump

You jump only once per turn, as the rope passes under your feet. Your feet remain on the ground as the rope comes over your head, but you may feel your body giving a little bounce from the knees up. That'll help balance you.

Two-Foot Jump

One-Foot Jump

One-Foot Jump

This is just what it sounds like. You lift one foot up behind you and take each jump with the other foot. This is very hard to keep up for any length of time.

Alternate-Foot Jump

You'll see why jumping is called skipping when you try this one. The first
time the rope passes under your feet,
jump with one foot. The other should
be slightly behind you and raised
higher off the ground
than the jumping foot.
Hold that pose for
your balancing hop,
then bring the raised
foot down and raise
the other foot for the
second hop. Keep
alternating feet.

Alternate-Foot Jump

One Step Further

Basic jumps are great for skipping to rhymes, but they're not going to satisfy you for long, so on to some fancier moves.

These may sound simple, but coordinating the rope swing with the footwork does take practice.

Before you try a new move, try the footwork without the rope. *Then* add it.

The instructions given are for a loner jumper, but you can also perform the steps while others turn the rope. There is a section at the end of each step called Speedy Review. Jump whenever the instructions read *"over rope."* If it doesn't say that, the move is made when the rope is over your head, not under your feet.

Run Step

For this step, you alternate one-foot balancing jumps with two-foot jumps. Jump first with both feet. As the rope swings up behind you, lift one foot up and slightly behind, as if about to run. As the rope comes down over your head, lower your foot so both feet take the jump together as the rope passes under your feet. When the rope swings back and up again, take off on the other foot.

Although, you look like you're running you won't move forward with the Run Step.

Speedy review:
> *Two-Foot Jump over rope*
> *Lift one foot*
> *Two-Foot Jump over rope*
> *Lift other foot*
> *Two-Foot Jump over rope*

Skip Step

This step takes the Alternate-Foot Jump one step further. After the rope passes under one foot, step forward with the other and take the next jump on the other leg. Keep moving forward with each jump. Depending on your

You can really move when you do the Skip Step.

speed, you'll end up walking, skipping or running forward. Just remember to look both ways at the corner, and send a postcard from wherever you end up.

Speedy review:
> *One-Foot Jump over rope*
> *Step*
> *One-Foot Jump over rope*
> *Step*

• • • • • • • • • • • • • • • •

A Skip to Far

Top hopper Vadivelu Karunakaren of India jumped 10 miles in 58 minutes in February 1990, with no breaks and no faults, using the skip step.

• • • • • • • • • • • • • • • •

Toe Tap

This is a fun, dancelike step. Use the Double Bounce as the base. Begin by jumping the rope once with two feet. As the rope passes up behind you, lift your right foot up slightly and swing it behind the left leg. Tap your

When jumping the Toe Tap, you cross one foot behind the other when tapping.

right toe on the ground just behind your left heel. Then swing your right foot back into position beside the left for the actual jump. On the next hop, tap the left toe in the reverse move.

Speedy review:

> Two-Foot Jump over rope
> Tap foot behind
> Two-Foot Jump over rope
> Tap other foot behind
> Two-Foot Jump over rope

Side Slide

Instead of moving your foot and tapping it behind you, you slide it out to the side.

The Side Slide is a version of the Toe Tap.

Make a two-Foot Jump first. Then, as the rope swings up, slide one foot out to the side and tap the ground. Quickly slide this foot back in time to make a Two-Foot Jump.

Speedy review:

> *Two-Foot Jump over rope*
> *Slide foot, tap*
> *Two-Foot Jump over rope*
> *Slide other foot, tap*
> *Two-Foot Jump over rope*

Heel Tap

Follow the instructions for the Toe Tap, but this time move one foot in *front* of the other and tap your heel on the ground in front of your other foot's toes.

Speedy review:
> *Two-Foot Jump over rope*
> *Tap heel in front*
> *Two-Foot Jump over rope*
> *Tap other heel in front*
> *Two-Foot Jump over rope*

For the Heel Tap you cross your feet in front to tap your heel.

Heel Click

This is a combination of the Slide Step and the Heel Tap. Again, you jump the rope with both feet. Instead

of a balancing hop you make this move: Lean over to the right and hop with both feet over to the left. Bend both knees and bring both heels together in a

You have to move fast to do the Heel Click.

click on the left. This will be a quick move, because you need to get both feet down again for the actual jump as the rope comes under your feet.

Your jump will be made with feet more widely spaced than normally, with your weight placed more heavily on the left foot. The next turn, lean to the left and click to the right.

Speedy review:
> *Two-Foot Jump over rope*
> *Click heels left*
> *Two-Foot Jump over rope*
> *Click heels right*
> *Two-Foot Jump over rope*

Split

This is a high-flying version of the gymnastic move. Jump with both feet together. Instead of following up with a balancing hop, jump high in the air, spreading your legs left and right or front and back. Drop in time to make a second Two-Foot Jump.

Speedy review:
> *Two-Foot Jump over rope*
> *Split*
> *Two-Foot Jump over rope*

March Step

The March Step is a combination of the Two-Foot Jump and the One-Foot Jump. Jump first with both feet together. The next jump is taken with one knee raised to bring one foot off the ground. Lower your leg for the next jump, which you take with both feet again. The next jump, bring up the other knee.

Try a small knee lift at first, then bring your knee up higher and higher with more practice.

Speedy review:
> *Two-Foot Jump over rope*
> *Lift one knee*
> *Two-Foot Jump over rope*
> *Lift other knee*
> *Two-Foot Jump over rope*

Up the Stairs

This is the March Step taken one step further. You drop the Two-Foot Jump and speed up the march. Jump with one knee up then quickly bring that leg down and raise the other for the next jump.

Speedy review:

>*Lift left knee, jump over rope*
>*Lift right knee, jump over rope*
>*Lift left knee, jump over rope*
>*Lift right knee, jump over rope*

With this version of the March Step you'll look like you're making a mad dash up the stairs.

Jumping Jacks

Turn the rope with your arms held out farther than usual. You'll take the first turn with a Two-Foot Jump. During the balancing hop, spread your legs wide in the classic Jumping Jack stance and make the second jump with your feet apart. The next jump is two-footed, the fourth with feet apart. Keep alternating these jumps.

Anyone who's ever done Jumping Jacks in gym class knows how this one goes.

Speedy review:

> *Two-Foot Jump over rope*
> *Spread legs and jump over rope*
> *Two-Foot Jump over rope*
> *Spread legs and jump over rope*

Criss-Cross

This one is like a dance step. It's a double bounce hop, but you make your balancing hop with your feet crossed. As the rope passes under your feet, jump with both feet. Then, as the rope comes up

For the Criss-Cross step, you'll cross your feet.

behind your back, cross one foot in front of the other and make a small, quick hop. As the rope passes in front of you, bring your foot back beside the other for the actual jump.

Speedy review:

> *Two-Foot Jump over rope*
> *Cross and uncross feet*
> *Two-Foot Jump over rope*
> *Cross and uncross feet*

Cross-Over

The Two-Foot Jump is the base. As the rope passes down in front of you and your arms are coming up and around, quickly cross one arm in front of the other. Your arms are crossed as the rope passes under your feet. As the rope comes down a second time, you uncross your arms so that the next jump is done normally.

In this variation your arms are the focus.

Speedy review:

> Two-Foot Jump over rope
> Cross arms
> Two-Foot Jump over rope over rope
> Uncross arms,
> Two-Foot Jump over rope

Scissors

In the Jumping Jack, you jumped every other turn with your feet apart. For Scissors, you jump once with your legs spread wide then quickly whip them back and across to take the next jump in a Criss-Cross.

Speedy review:

> *Spread legs and jump over rope*
> *Criss-Cross over rope*
> *Spread legs and jump over rope*
> *Criss-Cross over rope*

The Scissors is a combination of two moves, the Jumping Jack and the Criss-Cross.

Twist

Have you ever done the twist? Your upper body turns in one direction while your lower body and bent

Move over, Chubby Checker.

knees twist the opposite way. The jump itself is taken on both feet. Then swivel your knees over to one side while your upper body remains facing forward. Make a small balancing hop with your knees bent this way, then swing them forward for the actual jump. The next time, swivel your legs over in the opposite direction. You don't twist your upper body because that would make the rope loop warp too much for a jump.

Speedy review:
  Two-Foot Jump over rope
  Bend knees left
  Two-Foot Jump over rope
  Bend knees right

Kicks

That's right, you kick for this one.
Begin with a Two-Footed Jump, but
rest most of your weight on one foot.
As the rope is passing behind you,
lean on that foot and kick out with the
other, as high as
you like.

Speedy review:
  Two-Foot Jump over rope
  Kick
  Two-Foot Jump over rope
  Kick

*The Kick can be either
behind or in front of you,
small or very high.*

Cancan:

Dancers lift one knee high, lower it again to tap the toe and then kick the same leg is in the air. The jump rope

The Cancan is a favorite of the Rockettes and dance-hall girls everywhere.

version is very much the same. It's a combination of the Two-Foot Jump, the March Step and a Kick. The first jump is taken with both feet. The second jump raises one knee up in a March Step. The third jump swings the same leg straight up and out in a Kick. Then the Two-Foot Jump is jumped again and the other leg gets its turn.

Speedy review:

> *Two-Foot Jump over rope*
> *Bend left knee*
> *Two-Foot Jump*
> *Kick out left leg*
> *Two-Foot Jump over rope*
> *Bend left knee*
> *Two-Foot Jump*

Slalom

You begin with a two-foot jump. Then you make a balancing hop and land with both feet shifted slightly over to one side. Bring the feet center again to make the next jump. Don't try to shift too far over, or you may twist an ankle.

Speedy review:

> *Two-Foot Jump over rope*
> *Shift feet left,*
> *Two-Foot Jump over rope*
> *Shift feet right*
> *Two-Foot Jump over rope*

This move will seem familiar if you've ever hit the ski slopes.

Spin

This is a series of five moves that will take you in a circle. You make the first jump with two feet, facing forward. As the rope comes up, hop so you are facing right. After the jump, hop to your right another quarter turn so that you're now facing the opposite direction from the first jump. The next hop takes you another quarter turn, and the last one brings you to facing forward once again.

Speedy review:
> *Two-Foot Jump over rope*
> *Quarter turn*
> *Two-Foot Jump over rope*
> *Quarter turn*
> *Two-Foot Jump over rope*
> *Quarter turn*
> *Two-Foot Jump over rope*
> *Quarter turn*

Bet You Can't Do This

Actually, with lots of practice, bet you can! These two moves are truly tough—the Triple Axles of jumping rope—brought to you by some professional jumpers. If you master these, you've earned the black belt of skipping.

Bend Overs

This is a great one to end a routine with, because it comes to a stop when you're done. Begin by making a Two-Foot Jump. As the rope comes over your head, take a balancing hop with feet spread wide apart. Now, as the rope drops in front of you, bend over and cross your arms. The rope will close its loop and pass between your legs. When it does, stick your crossed arms between your legs and reach them out to either side as far as they'll go. Keep turning! The rope will pass over your bent head. When it reaches your feet again, jump. Then stand up and pull the rope back forward through your legs.

Speedy review:
> *Two-Foot Jump over rope*
> *Spread legs, bend, cross hands*
> *Pass rope between legs, no jump*
> *Stay bent, cross arms between and behind legs*
> *Two-Foot bent-over jump*
> *Stand*

Keep turning the rope when you're in this position to ▶
finish the Bend Over jump.

Pretzel

There's a reason for its name, and you're about to find it out. First, practice this stance without the rope: Raise one knee up as high as you can. Lean over and hook your arm under your raised knee. Not so easy? Now imagine doing it while jumping! Begin with a Two-Foot Jump. Then raise

In the pretzel, you jump first on one leg and then on the other.

your knee up as the rope comes up, jumping the next jump on just one leg. Immediately after the rope passes under your foot, hook your arm under your upraised leg, as you did

in the practice stance. The rope will
pass over your head in this pose. As
it drops in front of you, pull your arm
out from under your leg. Don't jump!
Instead swing the rope over to the
side, beside your legs. Stop there or,
as the rope comes up, shift your
hands to the front again so the rope
drops down under both feet. Jump two-
footed and start all over again.

Speedy review:
> *Two-Foot Jump over rope*
> *Bend knee to the side -*
> *One-Foot Jump over rope*
> *Hook arm behind legs, pull arm out*
> *Swing rope to one side*
> *Two-Foot Jump over rope*

Amaze your friends and neighbors!
Make up jump rope routines that
combine groups of these steps, ending with one of the last two. You'll be
the envy of the other jumpers on your
block if you ever get untwisted from
that pretzel!

CHAPTER 3

Jump Rope Jargon

Before learning the rhymes, you may want to bone up on some jump rope jargon. These are key words every good jumper knows, and they'll help you fit actions to the rhymes, since they crop up in the descriptions you'll find in this book. Even if you never get past Bluebells or if you never run into the wall, jump over the moon or over the waves, this jump rope jargon will make you sound like a champion jumper.

Loners Jumping rope alone with one's own rope

Starting in Place Jumper stands beside the rope as it rests on the ground; enders begin turning with the jumper already in position.

It takes perfect timing to run into the wall.

Running into the Wall Jumper runs into the rope as it is being turned *toward* the jumper.

Jumping Over the Moon Jumper runs into the rope as it is being turned *away* from the jumper

Double Dutch Style of turning using two enders with two ropes; the ropes alternate positions like the beaters on a mixer.

Stars Overhead Jumper crouches and enders raise the rope to turn it above the jumper's head; jumper then rises on cue from enders who simultaneously lower the rope. Timing is difficult, as jumper must stand just after rope passes overhead.

Salt Turning the rope as slowly as possible. Sometimes it may mean turning the rope at normal speed.

Pepper Rope is turned faster and faster and faster; there is no time for a balancing hop between passes.

Running Through (also called Through the tunnel) Jumpers run through the rope as it swings overhead, not allowing any part of their bodies to touch the rope.

Over the Waves Enders wiggle the ends of the rope up and down to create a wavelike pattern; rope begins a few inches from the ground but can then be raised higher and higher.

It's not easy to jump the snake.

Snake (also called Serpents)
Enders wiggle the ends of the rope back and forth to create a snaky pattern. Rope starts out a few inches from the ground but can than be raised higher and higher.

High Water/Low Water Enders pull the rope taut and hold it off the ground; rope begins a few inches from the ground and is raised higher and higher.

Up the Ladder/Down the Ladder

Jumper moves along the rope toward one ender in a series of jumps, then back down toward the other ender.

Back Door The position entering the rope as it is being turned away from the skipper

Front Door The position taken when entering the rope as it is being turned *toward* the skipper.

Bluebells (also called Rocking the cradle)

Rope is swung back and forth without being turned over-head; skippers must hop back and forth over the rocking rope.

Bluebells is often used at the beginnning of a rhyme.

This is trickier than it sounds!

CHAPTER 4

Rhymes to Start With

Don't wait until you've mastered all of jump rope's fancy steps before trying out some of these jump rope rhymes. Skipping to rhymes makes learning to jump a lot more fun. This chapter offers some basic rhymes that you can jump to with just about any step from basic to fancy. There are alphabet and number rhymes, fortune telling rhymes and nonsense rhymes, rhymes you complete and rhymes you build on. Does doing splits, spinning like a top and doing other stunts make you hop with excitement? There's a section of rhymes that let you show off your stuff.

Simple And Silly

Here are a few really easy jump rope rhymes to start with. Some are only two lines long, others are more. Because they are so simple, they let you experiment with footwork and speed. When you feel more confident, you can add a second and more complicated rhyme, jump to new rhymes and even make up your own.

You should supply the name of a friend—or foe—whenever you see this in a verse: (name).

Many jumpers begin with this classic verse:

Bluebells, cockle shells,
Evey ivey over.

The rope is rocked back and forth while the skipper jumps over it. At "over," the rope is swung over the head and regular jumping begins. You can use it to start any of the rhymes in this book.

A-N-T-A-R-C-T-I-C
(As you spell, turn the rope slowly.)
E-Q-U-A-T-O-R
(As you spell, turn the rope very fast.)

Forrest Gump sat on a stump.
He fell off and got a bump.

I like coffee, I like tea,
I like radio and TV.

I went downtown
To see Miss Brown.
She wore her
britches
Upside down.

Archie, Archie,
How about a date?
Meet me at the corner
At a quarter-past eight.

"I like coffee, I like tea..."

"K-I-S-S-I-N-G."

Here's a rhyme that you complete
using the names of people you know:

(Girl's name) and *(boy's name)* sittin'
in a tree.
K-I-S-S-I-N-G
First comes love, then comes marriage,
Then comes *(friend's name)* in a
baby carriage

*If skipping with more than one jumper, this rhyme
can be used as a running-in-and-out rhyme. Each
jumper chooses the name of a new skipper for the
"baby." After being named, the new skipper replaces
the old one.*

Cups and saucers,
Plates and dishes.
My old man
Wears calico britches.

Alphabet Rhymes

These rhymes are always changing because they rely on the jumper's imagination. The skipper continues supplying words down through the alphabet. It's pretty easy finding rhymes for letters like A, B, and C, but plan ahead for verses with letters like Q, X and Z.

Use these rhymes in group jumping, too. Each jumper recites a verse, so the rhyme keeps going and going and going . . .

A my name is Alice.
My husband's name is Adam.
We live in Alabama.
And we sell Apples.
B my name is . . .

I took a trip around the world,
And this is where I went:
From Africa to Boston,
From Boston to China,
From China to Detroit, . . .

My cat is an aristocratic cat.
My cat is a brave cat.
My cat is a careful cat . . .

Tick tock, tick tock,
Nine o'clock is striking.
Mother, may I go out?
All the boys are waiting.
One has an apple,
One has a bear,
One has a . . . .

*The skipper keeps adding gifts to the list in
alphabetical order.*

Two, Four, Six, Eight— Counting Rhymes

People have used numbers to begin rhymes since the beginning of jump rope rhymes. "Evey ivey over" came from an ancient one and two count. These rhymes all start with some kind of count. How they end . . . well, it ranges from sensible to downright silly.

Two, four, six, eight,
Meet me at the garden gate.
If you're late, I won't wait.
Two, four, six, eight.

One, two, three, four,
Skip and skip till you can't no more.
Five, six, seven, eight,
Skip and skip or you'll be late.
Nine, ten, start again.

One, two, three, four, five, six, seven,
All good children go to heaven.
Seven, six, five, four, three, two, one,
All bad children suck their thumbs.

"If you're late, I won't wait."

Shirley oneple
Shirley twople
Shirley threeple
Shirley fourple
Shirley fiveple
Shirley sixple
Shirley sevenple
Shirley eightple
Shirley nineple
Shirley Tenple

This is the way you
spell Tennessee:
One asee,
Two asee,
Three asee,
Four asee,
Five asee,
Six asee,
Seven asee,
Eight asee,
Nine asee,
Tennessee.

*"Shirley nineple
Shirley Tenple..."*

Crazy Mixed-up Rhymes

There are lots of nonsense rhymes like the following ones. Each has its own brand of mixed-up weirdness. Some don't make any sense at all, but that's the fun!

I went to the pictures next Tuesday
And took a front seat at the back.
I said to the lady behind me,
I can't see over your hat.
She gave me some well-broken cookies,
I ate them and gave her them back.
I fell from the pit to the balcony
And broke my front bone at the back.

The flowers were gaily singing,
The birds were in full bloom,
When I went to the cellar.
To look for an upstairs room.
I saw two thousand miles away
A house just out of sight.
It stood between two more,
Its walls were black all painted white.

Way down South where the bananas grow,
An ant stepped on an elephant's toe.
Then the elephant cried, with tears in his eyes,
"Pick on somebody your own darn size!"

"Ice cream, ice cream..."

Ice cream, ice cream,
Penny for a lump.
The more you eat
The more you jump.

I won't go to Macy's any more, more, more.
There's a great big policeman at the
Door, door, door.
He grabs you by the collar,
And makes you pay a dollar.
I won't go to Macy's any more, more, more.

Use the name of a store in your town.

'Twas midnight on the ocean,
Not a streetcar was in sight.
The sun was shining brightly
As it rained all day and night.
'Twas a summer day in winter,
And the snow was raining fast,
And a barefoot boy with his shoes on
Stood sitting in the grass.

Silly Stories

If you've ever listened to a story-teller spin a tale, you've heard a sing-song rhythm behind the words. Stories with repeating lines or sounds make good jump rope rhymes—the challenge is remembering them!

"Hello, hello, hello, sir."
"Meet me at the grocer."
"No, sir."
"Why, sir?"
"Because I have a cold, sir."
"Where'd you get your cold, sir?"
"At the North Pole, sir."
"Why were you there, sir?"
"I was watching Polar Bear, sir."
"Let me hear your sneeze, sir."
"Achoo, achoo, achoo, sir."

The skipper can add a line asking how many polar bears were seen, then begin counting for a 1-2-3 rhyme, or jump faster and faster until he or she misses.

Matthew, Mark, Luke and John
Went to bed with their trousers on.
Mark cried out in the middle of the night,
"Oh, my trousers are too tight!"

I went downtown and met Miss Brown.
She gave me a nickel, I bought a pickle.
The pickle was sour, I bought a flower.
The flower was red, I bought some thread.
The thread was thin, I bought a pin.
The pin was sharp, I bought a harp.
And on that harp I played . . . .

*Follow this with a song. You may also use it as a
lead-in to "Teddy Bear, Teddy Bear" or any other
action rhyme.*

"I went to the animal fair..."

I went to the animal fair.
All the birds and beasts were there.
The wild baboon by the light of the moon
Was combing his yellow hair.
The monkey fell from its bunk
And dropped on the elephant's trunk.
The elephant sneezed
And went down on its knees,
And what became of the monkey,
Monkey, monkey, monk?

There was a little fellow, dressed in white,
Wanted to go to Harvard on the tail of a kite.
The kite string broke and down he fell.
He didn't go to Harvard, he went to . . .
Now don't get excited and don't turn pale.
He didn't go to Harvard, he went to Yale.

There was a little fellow, his name was Jack.
He wanted to go to heaven in a Cadillac.
The carburetor broke and down he fell,
Instead of going to heaven he went to . . .
Now don't get excited, don't lose your head,
Instead of going to heaven, he went to bed.

Charlie Chaplin has big feet,
He thinks he owns the whole darn street.
If the street were made of glass,
Charlie would fall and break his . . .
Don't get excited, don't get alarmed,
Charlie Chaplin broke his arm.

This next rhyme was made up by kids a long time ago, using the names of towns in North Dakota and Minnesota. Try making up a rhyme using your local towns and landmarks, as this one does.

Up to Fargo with your cargo.
Down to Hibbing, stop your fibbing.
Up to Duluth, tell the truth.
Down the creek to catch some trout.
One, two, three, you'd better look out.

In *(your town's name)*
    there is a school,
In that school
    there is a class,
In that class
    there is a desk,
An in that desk
    there is a book,
And in that book
    there is a picture
And in that picture
    there is a *ghost!*

"Late last night and the night before..."

In the dark, dark world
There is a dark, dark, country.
In the dark, dark country
There is a dark, dark, wood.
In the dark, dark wood
There is a dark, dark house.
In the dark, dark house
There is a man trying to fix the fuse!

Late last night and the night before,
Twenty-four robbers
Came knockin' at my door.
I got up and let them in.
They knocked me on the head
With a rolling pin.

The skipper may add: "And this is what they said to me:" and follow it with another rhyme. Some skippers make this rhyme even sillier by replacing the twenty-four robbers with a lemon and a pickle.

Here is the rhyme that introduced us
to the lady with the alligator purse:

Miss Lucy had a baby,
His name was tiny Tim.
She put him in the bathtub
To see if he could swim.
He drank up all the water,
He ate up all the soap.
He tried to eat the bathtub,
But it got stuck in his throat.
Miss Lucy called the doctor,
Miss Lucy called the nurse,
Miss Lucy called the lady
With the alligator purse.
"Measles," said the doctor,
"Measles," said the nurse
"Mumps," said the lady
With the alligator purse.
Out goes the doctor, out goes the nurse,
Out goes the lady with the alligator purse.
And out goes YOU!

*If you have more than one skipper, three additional
jumpers can jump in and out for the doctor, nurse
and lady.*

Mother, Mother, I am sick,
Send for the doctor quick quick quick.
In came the doctor,
In came the nurse,
In came the lady with the alligator purse.
"Measles," said the doctor,
"Measles," said the nurse
"Nothing," said the lady
With the alligator purse.

Mother, Mother, may I go
Down to the meadow to see my beau?
No, my darling, you can't go
Down to the meadow to see your beau.
Father, Father, may I go
Down to the meadow to see my beau?
Yes, my darling, you may go
Down to the meadow to see your beau.
Mother said I could not go
Down to the meadow to see my beau.
You tell your mother to hold her tongue,
She had a beau when she was young.

Mother, Mother, Mother, pin a rose on me.
Two young men are in love with me.
One is blind and the other can't see.
Mother, Mother, Mother, pin a rose on me.

My mother said I never should
Play with the gypsies in the wood.
They tugged my hair and broke my comb.
I'll tell my mother when I get home.

Obediah jumped in the fire.
Fire so hot, jumped in a pot.
Pot so little, jumped in a kettle.
Kettle so black, jumped in a crack.
Crack so high, jumped to the sky.
Sky so blue, jumped in a canoe.
Canoe so shallow, jumped in the tallow.
Tallow so hard, jumped in the lard.
Lard so soft, jumped in the loft.
Loft so rotten, fell in the cotton.
Cotton so white, he stayed all night.

Rat-a-tat-tat, who is that?
Only grandma's pussy cat.
What do you want?
A pint of milk.
Where's your money?
In my pocket.
Where's your pocket?
I forgot it.
Oh, you silly pussy cat!

Standing at the corner,
Chewing bubble gum.
Along came a little boy
And asked me for some.
Oh, you dirty beggar!
Oh, you dirty bum!
Ain't you ashamed
To ask for bubble gum?

"Along came a little boy..."

Where are you going, Bill?
Downtown, Bill?
What for, Bill?
To pay my gas bill.
How much, Bill?
Ten-dollar bill.

Star Struck

These rhymes have been around in one form or another for years and years. Use the names of movie stars you admire and rhyme them if you can.

S-T-A-R
Roy Rogers is a star
Roy Rogers
Betty Grable
Rita Hayworth
Clark Gable

If you can't go to Hollywood,
You don't have to cry.
(Movie star's name) is good-looking
But so am I.

Mickey Mouse bought a house
Under an apple tree.
Mickey Mouse called his house
Number twenty-three.

The skipper counts from one to twenty-three, then begins again.

*"If you can't go to Hollywood,
you don't have to cry."*

CHAPTER 5

Fortune-Telling Rhymes

These are fortune-telling rhymes. Your miss-step predicts your future. Kind of a scary thought, no?

The way these rhymes work is by asking questions that are answered by skipping rope. When you miss, you've got your answer: yes or no, a number or letter. If jumping to the alphabet, you simply supply the name of someone or something with the initial letter you missed.

Will I Ever Catch a Fella?

Just about anyone who's ever jumped rope knows at least one version of the most famous fortune-telling rhyme, the one that asks the age-old question "Who is my true love?"

This section begins with the one popular version of that rhyme—complete with a number of burning follow-up questions. Other versions of this rhyme are scattered throughout this list.

Strawberry shortcake, cream on top
Tell me the name of my sweetheart:
A, B, C, D . . .
What kind of man will I marry?
Rich man, poor man, beggarman, thief,
      doctor, lawyer, Indian chief.

What day will we marry?
Monday, Tuesday, Wednesday . . .
What kind of place will we marry in?
Church, synagogue, temple, hall . . .
What color shirt will he wear?
Red, yellow, blue, green . . .
What kind of house will we live in?
House, shack, pig pen, castle . . .
What kind of dress will I marry in?
Silk, satin, calico, rags . . .
How many children will I have?
One, two, three, four . . .
Will my children behave themselves?
Yes, no, maybe so, yes, no, maybe so . . .

"Rich man, poor man, beggarman, thief..."

The "tinker, tailor" kind of fortune-telling rhyme is very old. One version of it was collected by a woman named Lady Gomme, back in 1898. Here are some of the choices jumpers were offered in her day:

Tinker, tailor, soldier, sailor,
Apothecary, ploughman, thief . . .
This year, next year, sometime, never . . .
Big house, little house, pigsty, barn . . .
Coach, carriage, wheelbarrow, dungcart . . .

Dungcart?!? Practice your skipping, because you don't want to trip on that one!

To add a little excitement while jumping to the following rhymes, the rope may be turned faster and faster until it reaches pepper speed.

I love my Papa, that I do,
And Mama says she loves him, too.
But Papa says he fears someday
With some bad man I'll run away.
Rich man, poor man, beggarman, thief,
Doctor, lawyer, Indian chief . . .

Mommy, Daddy, tell me true,
Who should I get married to?
John, Paul, George, Ringo

This version of the rhyme was recorded when
The Beatles were as hot as red hot peppers.
You can insert the names of your favorite rock stars.

Gypsy, gypsy, do not tarry,
Tell us when we two shall marry.
January, February, March . . .

The skipper then follows the pattern of "Strawberry
Shortcake."

Apples, peaches, pears and plums,
My true love's birthday in which month comes?
January, February, March . . .

Black currant, red currant, gooseberry jam,
What is the name of my young man?
A, B, C, D . . .

Ice cream soda, Delaware punch,
Spell me the name of my honeybunch.
A, B, C, D . . .

Ice cream soda, ginger ale, pop,
Give me the initial of my sweetheart.
A, B, C, D . . .

I love Bill, I love Larry,
I love Tom and Dick and Harry.
I love boys—now, let me see,
Which one will my boyfriend be?
A, B, C, D . . .

Strawberry shortcake, huckleberry pie,
Who's the apple of my eye?
A, B, C, D . . .

Strawberry, apple, my jam tart,
What's the name of my sweetheart?
A, B, C, D . . .

Sugar and cream,
Bread and butter,
What is the name of my true lover?
A, B, C, D . . .

Gypsy, gypsy, please tell me,
What my husband's name will be.
A, B, C, D . . .

Shame on me! Shame on me!
I've got a secret lover—
Don't even know his *(or her)* name.
Jump to find it—jump!
A, B, C, D . . .
He loves me—he don't.
He'll have me—he won't.
He would if he could—but he can't.
Does he love me?
Yes, no, maybe so, yes, no, maybe so . . .

He took her to the garden
And set her on his knee
And said, "Baby, please,
Won't you marry me?"
Yes, no, maybe so, yes, no, maybe so . . .

Blue and green, red and yellow,
Will I ever catch a fellow?
Yes, no, maybe so, yes, no, maybe so . . .

Blue and green, red and yellow,
Has your girl got another fellow?
Yes, no, maybe so, yes, no, maybe so . . .

I love coffee and I love tea,
I love the boys *(or girls)* and they love me!
Yes, no, maybe, yes, no, maybe so . . .

On the mountain stands a lady.
Who she is, I do not know.
All she wants is gold and silver.
All she wants is a nice young man.
Now then, *(skipper's name)*,
Don't tell lies,
We saw you kissing *(another name)*,
Round the corner.
How many kisses did you give?
One, two, three . . .
True, false, true, false, true . . .

Bread and butter,
Sugar and spice,
How many boys
Think I'm nice?
One, two, three . . .

My mother gave me a nickel,
My father gave me a dime,
My sister gave me a lover boy
Who kissed me all the time.
My mother took my nickel,
My father took my dime,
My sister took my lover boy
And left me Frankenstein.
He made me wash the dishes,
He made me scrub the floor.
I didn't like that one single bit,
So I kicked him out the door.
How many kicks did it take?
One, two three . . .

Down by the meadow,
Down by the sea,
I kissed Johnny and he kissed me.
One, two, three . . .

Ann is angry,
Bob is bad,
Helen is hateful,
Sam is sad.
I'm in love
And love is bliss.
How many times
Do I get a kiss?
One, two, three . . .

*"How many kisses did
he get in a week?"*

This version is more popular with boys:

Down in the meadow where
the green grass grows,
There sat *(boy's name)* in his old clothes.
He put his feet into the creek,
When along came *(girl's name)*
And kissed him on the cheek.
How many kisses did he get in a week?
One, two, three . . .

Down in the valley
Where the green grass grows,
There sat *(name)*,
Sweet as a rose.
Along came *(name)*
And kissed her on the cheek
How many kisses did she receive?
One, two, three . . .

Postman, postman, do your duty,
Take this letter to my cutie.
Postman, postman, don't delay,
Take it to him *(or her)* right away.
How many days will the letter take?
One, two, three . . .

Sister had a date last night.
Boyfriend held her very tight.
Brothers made a friendly bet.
How many kisses did she get?
One, two, three . . .

Come On, Quit Counting Already!

You would hate to be an ender when Park Bong Tae of South Korea begins a counting rhyme. Park broke the record for most consecutive jumps in an hour. He managed to cram 14,628 jumps into just 60 minutes. And, of course, he did it with no breaks and no faults.

"Postman, postman do your duty."

Cinderella

Cinderella sure gets around. There are a lot of jump rope rhymes where she is doing everything from raiding the refrigerator to buying umbrellas.

Most often, though, whether she's dressed in blue or yellow, whether she's downtown or upstairs, eating ice cream or fussing with her footwear, Cinderella's smooching with somebody.

Cinderella, dressed in yella,
Went upstairs to kiss a fella.
How many kisses did she receive?
One, two, three . . .

Cinderella, dressed in yella,
Went upstairs to kiss a fella.
Made a mistake and kissed a snake,
Came downstairs with a bellyache.
How many doctors did it take?
One, two, three . . .

You can catch Cinderella kissing TV characters and other people, wearing colors to match.

Cinderella, dressed in purple,
Went upstairs to kiss Steve Urkel . . .

Cinderella, dressed in brown
Went upstairs to kiss a clown.

"Cinderella dressed in purple went upstairs to kiss Steve Urkell."

Cinderella, dressed in yella,
Went downtown to buy an umbrella.
On the way she met a fella.
How many kisses did she receive?
One, two, three . . .

And Cinderella is apparently quite a
fashion plate—these just go on and on:

Cinderella,
Dressed in red,
Went downstairs
To bake some bread.
How many loaves
Did she bake?
One, two, three . . .

Cinderella,
Dressed in blue,
Went outside
To tie her shoe.
How many seconds
Did it take?
One, two, three . . .

"Cinderella, dressed in yella."

Cinderella, dressed in green,
Went upstairs to eat ice cream.
How many scoops did she have?
One, two, three . . .

Cinderella, dressed in lace,
Went upstairs to powder her face.
How many powder puffs did she use?
One, two, three . . .

Cinderella, dressed in silk,
Went downstairs to drink some milk.
How many glasses did she drink?
One, two, three . . .

Cinderella, dressed in blue,
Went upstairs to find her shoe.
How many slippers did she find?
One, two, three . . .

Cinderella, dressed in black,
Went upstairs and sat on a tack.
How many stitches did it take?
One, two, three . . .

One, Two, Three

There are hundreds of counting rhymes that begin as a story and end with the question of how many: How many pieces of bubble gum or mail, how many bricks or dishes or peas. If you can count 'em, they're in a jump rope rhyme.

Counts are jumped to a rollicking stint of red hot pepper in which the jumper speed-skips until he or she misses. Try these and then make up your own counting rhymes. How high can *you* go?

Abraham Lincoln was no crook
Because his nose was always in a book.
How many books did he read?
One, two, three . . .

Bubble gum, bubble gum, in a dish
How many pieces do you wish?
One, two, three . . .

Little Georgie Washington never told a lie,
Because he was eating cherry pie.
How many cherries in the pie?
One, two, three . . .

Every morning at eight o'clock,
You can hear the postman's knock.
Postman, postman, drop the mail.
Lady, lady, pick it up.
How many letters did she pick up?
One, two, three . . .

*With each jump, the skipper must touch the ground,
as if picking up the mail.*

Grandmother, grandmother, tell me the truth,
How many years have I been in school?
One, two, three . . .

I eat my peas with honey,
I've done it all my life,
It makes the peas taste funny
But keeps them on my knife.
How many peas stick on my knife?
One, two, three . . .

I had a little sister,
Dressed in pink.
She washed all the dishes
In the sink.
How many dishes did she break?
One, two, three . . .

I know a Scout who
took me out.
He gave me chips to
Grease my lips.
How many kisses
Did he get?
One, two, three . . .

I like to jump,
I like to bump,
If I fall
I'll get a lump.
How many lumps
Will I get?
One, two, three . . .

"I had a little sister..."

I was born in a frying pan.
Can you guess how old I am?
One, two, three . . .

I was taking a wee little piggy
Down to the animal fair.
He grew into a great big hog
Before we ever got there.
How many pounds did he weigh?
One, two, three . . .

Lickety, lickety, lickety split.
How many times before I quit?
One, two, three . . .

Mabel, Mabel, set the table.
Company's coming for dinner.
How many people will there be?
One, two, three . . .

Mickey Mouse built a house.
How many bricks did he need?
One, two, three . . .

Mother runs the butcher shop,
Father cuts the meat.
I'm just their little kid
Running 'cross the street.
How many times do I cross?
One, two, three . . .

Mrs. Drake made a cake.
The cake was soggy,
She fed it to her doggy.
The doggy ate the cake,
He got the stomachache.
How many days did he have it?
One, two, three . . .

My mother made a chocolate cake.
How many eggs did she break?
One, two, three . . .

My mother's going to have a baby.
Will it be twins, triplets, boys or girls?
Twins, triplets, boys, girls, twins, triplets . . .

My old granddad made a shoe.
How many nails did he put through?
One, two, three . . .

My teacher is crazy.
She joined the navy
When she was
One, two, three . . .

Popeye went down in the cellar
To drink some spinach juice.
How many gallons did he drink?
One, two, three . . .

"Mrs. Drake made cake . . ."

"peaches in the parlor,"

(Name) did the washing up.
(Name) broke a coffee cup.
How much will it cost?
One cent, two cents, three cents . . .

Now you're married
And you must be good.
Make your husband
Chop the wood.
Count your children
One by one:
One, two, three . . .

One, two, three, four, five, six, seven,
All good children go to heaven.
If you're bad you cannot go,
All the rest go down below.
How many bad ones go below?
One, two, three . . .

Peaches in the parlor,
Apples on the shelf.
(Skipper's name) is getting tired
Of skipping by herself.
How many skips did she skip by herself?
One, two, three . . .

Pitch, patch, patch my britches.
How many stitches?
One, two, three . . .

Powder box, powder box, powder your nose.
How many petals are in a rose?
One, two, three . . .

Salt, pepper, vinegar, cider.
How many legs has a bow-legged spider?
One, two, three . . .

Tell me, tell me, tell me true,
How old, how old, how old are you?
One, two, three . . .

The sailor went to sea sea sea
To see what he could see see see,
But all that he could see see see
Was the bottom of the deep blue sea sea sea.
How many days was he seasick?
One, two, three . . .

"Tell me, tell me, tell me true."

A, B, C, D

Alphabet rhymes operate the same way counting rhymes do. Try them all and then make up some of your own.

What shall I name my little pup?
I'll have to make a good one up.
A, B, C, D . . .
Skipper picks a name with the letter missed.

Teacher nearly had a fit
When I learned the alphabet.
Seems I wasn't very bright—
I could never get it right.
I always got stuck after
A, B, C, D . . .

My name is Santa Claus.
I bring lots of toys
To little girls and boys
Whose names begin with
A, B, C, D . . .

If I could change my name-us,
I would soon be famous.
What would I change it to?
A, B, C, D . . .

A, B, C and all that goop.
What will I find in my alphabet soup?
A, B, C, D . . .

The skipper thinks up something odd that begins with the letter that was missed.

CHAPTER 6

Sort-Of-Sick Rhymes

These rhymes are either gross, morbid, bizarre, or just plain mean. They're also some of the most popular. A lot of them are very old, too. I guess that means your grandparents were just as sick as you are!

OoPS!

Vomiting is a theme that appears quite often in sick rhymes. Here are a few with a high yuck factor to add to your repertoire.

Regurgitate, regurgitate,
Throw up all the food you ate.
Ralph! Ralph! Vomit!

Apple, apple on a stick,
Five cents a lick.
Every time I turn around,
It makes me sick.

Hop around in a circle during third line,
then pretend to throw up.

Lincoln, Lincoln,
I been thinkin'.
What in the world have you been drinkin'?
Smells like liquor, tastes like wine,
Oh, my gosh, it's turpentine.
How many bottles did you drink?
One, two, three . . .

Quick, quick,
The cat's been sick.
Where, where?
Under the chair.
Hasten, hasten,
Get the basin.
No, no,
Get the bowl.
(name), *(name)*, you're far too late,
The carpet's in a dreadful state.

Margie drank some marmalade,
Margie drank some pop,
Margie drank some other things
That made her stomach flop.
Whoops, went the marmalade,
Whoops, went the pop,
Whoops, went the other things
That made her stomach flop.
(Make a disgusting gagging noise at each Whoops.)

Sally ate a pickle,
Sally ate some pie,
Sally ate some sauerkraut,
Sally thought she'd die.
Oops, says the pickle,
Oops, says the pie,
Oops, says the sauerkraut
That made Sally think she'd die.
(Skipper pretends to throw up at each Oops.)

I See London, I See France

So many of the sick rhymes have to do with seeing someone's underwear or losing underwear or just wearing underwear. No wonder your mom is always telling you to wear a clean pair.

I see London,
I see France,
I see *(name)*'s
    underpants,

Teacher, teacher,
    I declare
I see *(name)*'s
    underwear!

*"Teacher, teacher,
I declare . . ."*

139

Tarzan, Tarzan, in the air,
Tarzan lost his underwear.
Tarzan say, "Me no care,
Jane make me 'nother pair."
Jane, Jane, in the air,
Jane lost her underwear.
Jane say, "Me no care,
Cheetah make me 'nother pair."
Cheetah, Cheetah, in the air,
Cheetah lost his underwear.
Cheetah say, "Me no care,
Cheetah need no underwear."

The King of France
Wet his pants,
Right in the middle
Of a wedding dance.
How many puddles did he make?
On, two, three . . .

(Name) has no underpants,
Will you loan her *(or him)* yours, by chance?
(Name) is going far away,
To sing ta-ra-ra-boom-de-ay!

Cinderella dressed in yellow
Went downtown to buy some Jell-O.
On the way her girdle busted.
How many people were disgusted?
One, two, three . . .

Marilyn Monroe
Fell in the snow.,
Her skirt blew up
And the boys said "Oh!"

Dream lover, where did you go?
Upstairs by the toilet bowl.
Whatcha doing way up there?
Washing out my underwear.
How'd you get them so squeaky clean?
With a bottle of Listerine.

Oh, Gross!

These rhymes are just plain disgusting. They're about creepy bugs, breaking bones, drowning, and other morbid things. How many do you recognize?

"Doctor, Doctor, tell me quick, how many times will I be sick..."

I was standing on the corner,
Not doing any harm,
Along came a policeman
Who took me by the arm.
He took me round the corner,
And he rang a little bell.
Along came a police car
And took me to my cell.
I woke up in the morning
And looked up at the wall.
The cooties and the bedbugs
Were playing a game of ball.
The score was six to nothing,
The bedbugs were ahead.
The cooties hit a homerun,
And knocked me out of bed.

The parson in the pulpit
Couldn't say his prayers.
He gabbled and he gobbled
Till he tumbled down the stairs.
The stairs gave a crack,
And he broke his poor old back,
And all the congregation
Gave a quack, quack, quack.

A bug and a flea
Went out to sea
Upon a reel of cotton.
The flea was drowned
But the bug was found,
Biting a lady's bottom.

I went downtown
To the alligator farm.
I sat on the fence
And the fence broke down.
The alligator bit me
By the seat of my pants
And made me do
The hula hula dance.

There was an old woman
And her name was Pat.
And when she died,
She died like that.
(Skipper jumps with hands crossed on chest like a corpse)
They put her in a coffin
And she fell out the bottom
Just like that.
(Skipper falls to the ground)

Doctor, doctor, tell me quick,
How many days will I be sick?
One, two, three . . .
Doctor, Doctor, tell no lie,
How many days before I die?
One, two, three . . .

Mother, Mother, I feel sick.
Call the doctor, quick, quick, quick.
Doctor, doctor, will I die?
Yes, my dear and so will I.
How many hearses will there be?
One, two, three . . .

Mrs. Red went to bed.
In the morning she was dead.

When you grow up
And think you're so sweet,
Take off your shoes
And smell your feet!

Fudge, Fudge, someone call the judge.
(Name) is having a baby.
Wrap it up in tissue paper,
Put it in the elevator.
How many floors did it go up?
first floor, second floor, third floor . . .

Judge, judge, tell the judge,
Mamma has a newborn baby.
It's a boy, full of joy,
Papa's going crazy.
Wrap it up in tissue paper,
Send it down the elevator.
How many pounds did it weigh?
One, two, three . . .
*(At each number, enders may turn the rope
higher and higher)*

Two little monkeys
Jumping on the bed.
One fell off and broke his head.
Took him to the doctor
And the doctor said,
"That's what you get for jumping on the bed."

Cinderella, dressed in bows,
Went upstairs to blow her nose.
How many boogers did she make?
One, two, three . . .
How many tissues did it take?
One, two, three . . .

Albert, Albert, in the tub.
Mother forgot to put in the plug.
Oh my heart, oh my soul,
There goes Albert down the hole.

"Albert, Albert, in the tab"

This one's a gag that works only once with each friend, so use it wisely:

A apple pie
B baked it
C cut it
D divided it
E eat it
F fought for it
G got it
H hit at it
I eyed it
J jumped at it
K kicked at it
L longed for it
M mourned for it
N nodded at it
O opened it
Q quartered it
R run for it
S turned it
U earned it
V viewed it
W wanted it
XYZ got in and run off to eat it.
*(Someone will ask you, "Hey, what happened to P?"
Then you say, "There's none on me." Get it?)*

Just plain Mean

These rhymes are downright nasty.
Mean, mean, mean!

Teacher, teacher, oh so tired,
How many times have you been fired?
One, two, three . . .

"How many times have you been fired?"

As I was walking down the street,
I heard my boyfriend say
To the little Dutch girl
Who lives across the way:
I L-O-V-E love you
I K-I-S-S kiss you
On your C-H-E-E-K.
As I was walking down the street,
I heard my boyfriend say
To the little Dutch girl
Who lives across the way:
I H-A-T-E hate you.
I K-I-C-K kick you
On your B-U-T-T butt!

Been in Grandad's garden,
Turned on the garden hose.
How many times will Grandad
Punch me in the nose?
One, two, three . . .

Doctor Brown fell in the well,
Broke his collar bone.
Why don't he tend to the sick,
And leave the well alone?

Tonight, tonight, a pillow fight,
Tomorrow is the end of school
Break the dishes, break the chairs,
Trip the teachers on the stairs.

Glory, glory, hallelujah,
Teacher hit me with a ruler.
I conked him on the bean,
With a rotten tangerine,
Now teacher won't teach
No more, more, more.

God made *(name)*,
But we all make mistakes!
(On mistakes the skipper misses.)

I had a little monkey
Dressed in red.
Along came a train
And knocked him dead.
*(At dead, skipper stops the rope by deliberately
missing)*

I should worry, I should care,
I should marry a millionaire.
He should die, I should cry,
Then I'd marry another guy.

"I should worry, I should care..."

I'd rather scrub the dishes,
I'd rather scrub the floor,
I'd rather kiss the garbage man
Than kiss *(name)* behind the door.

I'm a little girl just so high.
I tried to eat the pumpkin pie.
Broke the platter right in two.
Mother came to spank me, boo hoo hoo.
How many spankings did I get?
One, two, three . . .

I'm a pretty little Dutch girl,
As pretty as can be.
All the boys around the block
Are crazy over me.
My boy friend's name is Michael,
He rides a motorcycle,
With a pimple on his nose
And ten flat toes.
And that's the way my story goes.

Jeepers, creepers, chimney sweeper
Had a wife and couldn't keep her.
Had another, didn't love her.
Up the chimney he did shove her.

(President's name) is in the White House,
Waiting to be elected,
(Former president's name) is in the garbage,
Waiting to be collected.

Johnny gave me apples,
Johnny gave me pears,
Johnny gave me fifty cents
And kissed me on the stairs.
I gave him back his apples,
I gave him back his pears,
I gave him back his fifty cents
And kicked him down the stairs.
How many stairs did he fall down?
One, two, three . . .

Johnny on the ocean,
Johnny on the sea,
Johnny broke a milk bottle
and blamed it all on me.
I told Ma, Ma told Pa,
Johnny got a whipping,
Ha ha ha!
How many whippings did he get?
One, two, three . . .

Julius Caesar,
The Roman geezer,
Squashed his wife
With a lemon squeezer.

My great big ball
Went over the wall.
So mother dear
She slapped my rear.
R-E-A-R, rear.

CHAPTER 7

Going Solo

Action Rhymes
for One Jumper

You can skip loners to the rhymes you've already read, or try your feet on something a little more challenging. These are rhymes that make you run, jump, kick, spin, watusi and do a midair split. Most are for one jumper with two enders, but you can use them while jumping loners, too—just substitute kicks and other fancy hops for the actions you can't do alone. If there is more than one jumper, each can take a turn at the rhyme.

Hopping and Splitting

Many rhymes have directions built right in. Here are a bunch that involve all sorts of hopping and jumping and splitting. The first one is an oldie. It can be sung before one of the other, more complicated, action rhymes:

As I went down to my grandfather's farm,
A billygoat chased me 'round the barn
(Skipper runs out of rope and around an ender, then back into the rope.)
It chased me up a sycamore tree
(Skipper skips Up the Ladder.)
And this is what it said to me:
(Skipper jumps along to the words of a popular rhyme such as Teddy Bear, Teddy Bear.)

Wavy, wavy, turn the rope over,
Mother's at the butcher's buying fresh meat.
Baby's in the cradle, playing with a rattle.
Sister's at the table, eating all she's able.

Enders begin by making waves; the skipper must hop back and forth. At "over," the enders bring the rope up and over and begin turning.

Donald Duck is a one-legged, one-legged, one-legged duck.
(Skipper jumps on one leg.)

Donald Duck is a two-legged, two-legged, two-legged duck.
(Skipper jumps with both feet.)

Donald Duck is a three-legged, three-legged, three-legged duck.
(Skipper touches the ground with one hand with each Two-Foot Jump.)

Donald Duck is a four-legged, four-legged, four-legged duck.
(Skipper touches the ground with both hands with each Two-Foot Jump.)

Donald Duck is a bow-legged, bow-legged, bow-legged duck.
(Skipper jumps with knees turned out.)

Donald Duck is a knock-kneed, knock-kneed, knock-kneed duck.
(Skipper jumps with knees turned in.)

Donald Duck is a pigeon-toed, pigeon-toed, pigeon-toed duck.
(Skipper jumps with toes turned in. Continue the rhyme with any other funny jumps you can think of.)

Lady on your one foot, one foot, one foot.
Lady on your two feet, two feet, two feet.
Lady on your three feet, three feet, three feet.
Lady on your four feet, four feet, four feet.

*Skipper jumps first on one foot, then on both feet,
then on both feet and touching the ground with one
hand, then on both feet and touching the ground
with two hands.*

"Lady on your one foot, one foot, one..."

Little Orphan Annie
Jumps on one foot, one foot.
Little Orphan Annie
Jumps on two feet, two feet.
Little Orphan Annie
Jumps on three feet, three feet.
Little Orphan Annie
Jumps on four feet, four feet.
Little Orphan Annie
Jumps O-U-T out.

Peel an orange round and round
Peel a banana upside down.
If you can count to twenty-four,
You may have an extra turn.

Skipper jumps in a circle in first one direction then the other. During the count, the enders turn at pepper speed, then the rhyme begins again.

Hurry, hurry, don't be late.
Meet us at the garden gate.
Jump it high.
Jump it low.
Turn around and out you go.

The enders follow the directions: raising the rope and lowering it. Then the skipper jumps in a circle inside the rope and finally runs out.

This is the way you spell Mississippi:
Capital M, I,
Crooked letter, crooked letter, I,
Crooked letter, crooked letter, I,
Hunchback, hunchback, I.

*Skipper jumps pigeon-toed for M, with feet tight
together for I, and with one knee up for the "hunchback" P .*

I see Peter
On the heater.
Ding, dong!
The fire bell.
Up the ladder, down the ladder,
Ding, dong bell.

*Skipper jumps up and down the ladder,
over and over.*

There came a girl from France,
There came a girl from Spain,
There came a girl from the USA,
And this is how she came:
Hopping on one foot . . .
Skipper jumps a series of fancy steps.

I had a dolly
Dressed in green.
I didn't like her,
I gave her to the queen.
The queen didn't like her,
Gave her to the king.
Close your eyes and
count sixteen.

*The skipper jumps sixteen
times with closed eyes.*

*"Close your eyes and
count to sixteen."*

"Father, Father, give me
the key."
*(Skipper jumps up the ladder while chanting the first
line. The ender there sings the next line:)*
"Go to your mother."
*(Skipper jumps back down the ladder while chanting
the third line. That ender chants the fourth line.)*
"Mother, Mother, give me the key."
"Go to your father."
Skipper jumps back and forth, back and forth.

Old lady, old lady,
Lived in a shoe.
Old lady, old lady,
What to do?
Old lady, old lady,
Stubbed her toe.
Skipper taps toe.
Old lady, old lady,
Out you go!
Skipper runs out.

Old Miss Daisy,
She drives me crazy.
Up the ladder,
Down the ladder,
Over my head,
One, two, three,
Salt, vinegar, pepper!

*"Old lady, old lady,
stubbed her toe."*

*Skipper jumps up and down the ladder, then crouches
as the rope is turned over the moon. At "pepper'" the
enders turn the rope as fast as they can.*

Anna Banana
Plays the pianna.
All she knows is "The Star Spangled Banner."
Banana, banana, banana split!

*Skipper does a split on "split" or tries three in a row,
one for each "banana" in the last line.*

Banana, banana,
Banana split,
Went to the drugstore
To get a banana split.
One banana, two banana,
Three banana splits!

*Skipper does three splits
on the last line, with a
balancing hop or two
between each.*

"Banana, banana,
banana split."

Teddy Bear, Teddy Bear

This rhyme is one everybody seems to know. "Teddy Bear" and its variations put skippers through a marathon of jumps and fancy steps. Skippers hop in a circle, tap the ground, slap a shoe, bow, jump with knees up, and mime all the actions before running out of the rope at "goodnight."

"...touch your toe."

This kind of rhyme is fun when everyone chants it and the jumper adds a special touch to each move—

"...touch the ground."

the sillier, the better. But these rhymes are also fun if only the enders chant it, slipping in new verses or a different order so the jumper doesn't know what's coming.

"..turn around."

Teddy bear, teddy bear,
Turn around.
Teddy bear, teddy bear,
Touch the ground.
Teddy bear, teddy bear,
Shine your shoe.
Teddy bear, teddy bear,
Say how do you do.
Teddy bear, teddy bear,
Go up the stairs.
Teddy bear, teddy bear,
Say your prayers.
Teddy bear, teddy bear,
Turn out the light.
Teddy bear, teddy bear,
Say goodnight.

You can also use these words instead of "Teddy bear, teddy bear."

Anda Panda
Butterfly, butterfly
Lady, lady
Buster, buster

There are other versions of this famous rhyme. Try to perform all of the actions.

Ladybug, ladybug,
Turn around.
Ladybug, ladybug,
Touch the ground.
Ladybug, ladybug,
Point to the sky.
Ladybug, ladybug,
Show your glass eye.
Ladybug, ladybug,
You have gone.
Ladybug, ladybug,
Fly away home.

Bubble gum, bubble gum, chew and blow.
Bubble gum, bubble gum, scrape your toe.
Bubble gum, bubble gum, tastes so sweet.
Get that bubble gum off your feet.

I'm a little Dutch girl dressed in blue.
These are the things I like to do:
Salute to the captain,
Bow to the queen,
Turn my back on the yellow submarine.

*Skipper performs the actions named, then hops
around to face the opposite direction on the last line.*

"Salute the captain."

Dolly Dimple walks like this.
Dolly Dimple talks like this.
Dolly Dimple smiles like this.
Dolly Dimple throws a kiss.

Cobbler, cobbler, fix my shoe.
Have it ready by half past two.
If half past two is far too late,
Have them ready by half past eight.
One, two, three, four.
Back two, three, four.
Glue it, shoe it, hammer, hammer, hammer.

*Skipper jumps up and down the ladder while counting
one through four twice. Then, at "hammer," the enders
turn the rope at pepper speed.*

Red, white and blue,
Tap me on the shoe.
Red, white and green,
Tap me on the bean.

Little Sally Water,
Sitting in a saucer.
Rise, Sally, rise,
Wipe off your eyes.
Put your hand on your hip,
Don't let your backbone slip.
Turn to the East, Sally,
Turn to the West.
Turn to the one, Sally,
That you love best.

*The skipper starts by crouching, then rises and mimes
the actions described. The skipper hops to face one
direction then the other for "east" and "west," then
hops to face an ender on the last line. The ender
becomes the next to skip.*

Policeman, policeman, stop that thief!
Make him jump without relief.
Make him jump and kick his feet,
Make him jump 'til he is beat.
Make him jump and tap his nose,
Make him jump and click his toes,
And when it's almost time for supper,
Make him jump like red hot pepper.

Mademoiselle went to the well,
Combed her hair and brushed it well.
She jumped up high and touched the sky
And twirled around until she dropped.
My left hand, my right hand,
Touch my knee,
Touch my heel,
Touch my toe,
And under I go.

*At "hand," skipper jumps to face first left, then right,
then follows the next three actions. At "under," the
skipper ducks under the rope and runs out.*

Oliver Jump
Oliver Jump
Oliver Jump jump jump.
Oliver Kick
Oliver Kick
Oliver Kick kick kick.
Oliver Twist
Oliver Twist
Oliver Twist twist twist.
Oliver Jump jump jump.
Oliver Kick kick kick.
Oliver Twist twist twist.

Oliver Twist, he can't do this,
So what's the use of trying?
Number one: Touch your tongue.
Number two: Touch your shoe.
Number three: Bend your knee.
Number four: Touch the floor.
Number five: Wave good-bye.
Number six: Do the splits.
Good-bye, Oliver Twist.
(Skipper runs out on the final line.)

One, two, buckle my shoe.
Three, four, kick the door.
Five, six, pick up sticks.
Seven, eight, stays out late.
Nine, ten, back in again!
(Skipper jumps out and in on cue.)

Cowboy Joe from Mexico,
Hands up, stick 'em up,
Drop your guns
And pick 'em up.
Cowboy Joe from Mexico.

"Hands up, stick 'em up."

Skipper sticks hands up in the air, then stoops to touch the ground.

With my hands on myself, what have I here?
This is my brainbox, nothing to fear.
(Skipper taps head.)
Brain-box and a wiggy-waggy-woo,
That's what they taught me when
I went to school.
With my hands on myself, what have I here?
This is my eye-blinker, nothing to fear.
(Skipper taps closed eyelids.)
Eye-blinker, brain-box and a wiggy-waggy-
woo,
That's what they taught me when I went to
school.
*(Skipper goes on repeating
the pattern, tapping each
body part while reciting that
verse.)*
nose-wiper
(hand wipes nose)
mouthclicker *(teeth)*
chin-chopper *(jaws)*
chest-protector
(breastbone)
breadbox *(stomach)*
knee-benders *(knees)*

"...what have I here?"

With my hands on myself, what have I here?
These are my globe-trotters *(feet)*, nothing to fear.
Globe-trotters, knee-benders,
Bread-box, chest-protector,
Chin-chopper,mouth-clicker,
Nose-wiper, eye-blinker,
Brain-box and a wiggy-waggy-woo,
That's what they taught me
when I went to school.

"nose wiper . . ."

Shimmy, Shimmy

There's a whole lotta shakin' goin
on in these action rhymes, with
shimmies, wiggles, wag-
gles rhumbas, hootchie
cootchies and kicks. So
put on your dancing
shoes—or sneakers—
and try one of these.

Jelly in the bowl,
Jelly in the bowl.
Wiggle waggle,
Wiggle waggle,
Jelly in the bowl.

"wiggle waggle."

Hello, boys, do you want to flirt?
Here comes *(name)* in a calico skirt.
She can wiggle, she can jiggle,
She can do the splits.
She can pull her skirt up to her hips.

Hey, *(celebrity's name)*,
how about a date?
Meet me at the corner at
half past eight.
I can do the rhumba,
I can do the splits,
I can do the turn-around,
And I can do the kicks.

"she can wiggle."

Ladies and gentlemen,
Children, too,
This young lady's going to
    boogie for you.
She's going to turn
    around,
She's going to touch
    the ground,
She's going to shimmy
shimmy shimmy till her
drawers fall down.
She never went to college,
She never went to school,
But when she came back
    she was a nasty fool.

"she can jiggle."

Lady in the tight skirt
Can't do this:
(Skipper chooses and
performs an action.)
Lady in the tight skirt
Can't do this:
(Skipper continues
choosing different actions
and steps.)

"Lady in a tight skirt can't
do this."

Marco Polo went to
France
To teach the ladies how to dance.
Heel and toe and around we go.
Cross your legs and out you go.
(Skipper taps a heel, then a toe, spins around,
crosses feet and then runs out of the rope.)

Here's a version of "Marco Polo" that boys prefer to chant:

Marco Polo went to France
To teach the men there how to dance.
First a kick and then a bow,
Marco Polo showed them how.

My mother is a dancer,
Brother, can she twist.
She can do the hootchie cootchie,
Just like this.
She can do the can-can,
She can do the split,
She can do the tap dance,
Just like this.

*Skipper performs dance steps. The for the last line,
skipper taps heel and toe.*

Policeman, policeman,
do your duty,
Here comes *(name)*,
the American beauty.
She can dance,
she can sing,
She can do most
anything.

*The skipper chooses a
fancy step for the
last line.*

"Marco Polo went to
France . . ."

Policeman, policeman,
Do your duty.
Here comes *(name)*, an American beauty.
She can wiggle, she can waggle,
She can do the twist.
But I bet you any money
That she can't do this.

Skipper chooses any fancy step to end with.

Red, white and blue,
Stars shine over you.

At "over," the enders lift rope and turn it above the skipper, who crouches. Then the skipper rises and the enders lower the rope to normal skipping height.

"she can do the twist."

Salome was a dancer;
She danced before the king,
And every time she danced,
She wiggled everything.
"Stop!" said King Herod.
"You cannot do that here."
Salome said, "Baloney!"
And kicked the chandelier.

Spanish dancer,
Do the splits,
Spanish dancer,
Do high kicks,
Spanish dancer,
Do the rounds,
Spanish dancer,
Touch the ground,
Spanish dancer,
Get out of town.

Skipper runs out on last line.

"Salome was a dancer;"

Be A Bungler:
Rhymes That Make You Miss

These rhymes are favorites for jumpers with two left feet. They ask you to miss on demand. At the cue in italics, the skipper stops the rope by stepping on it, grabbing it, or trying to get tangled in it some other creative way.

Andy, Mandy,
Sugar candy,
Now's the time to miss.

I had a doll, her name was Sis,
My doll Sis would miss like *this*.

I had a little car in 1988,
Went around the corner
And slammed on the *brake*.

Dolly Dimple walks like this.
(Skipper does a fancy step)
Dolly Dimple talks like this.
*(Skipper talks nonsense or sings
a short rhyme or song.)*
Dolly Dimple throws a kiss.
(Skipper mimes the action.)
Dolly Dimple misses like *this*.

I know a little lady, and her name is Miss.
She went around the corner to buy some fish.
She met a fellow and she gave him a kiss.
I know a little lady, and her name is *Miss*.

I know a man, his name is Mister,
He knows a lady, and her name is *Miss*!

Jump and miss, jump and miss,
When I jump rope, I miss like *this*.
Jump rope, jump rope,
Will I miss?
Jump rope, jump rope,
Just watch *this*.

Little Miss Pinky, dressed in blue,
Died last night at half-past two.
Before she died, she told me this:
"Let the jump rope miss like *this*."

CHAPTER 8

Two In the Middle

Action Rhymes for More Than One Jumper

When there's a string of jumpers all wanting to skip, things can get a little hairy. Here are some rhymes that are great for a crowd. Some keep the line moving, replacing one jumper with the next and the next. Others keep piling on the skippers until the rope is so crowded, there's hardly room to jump.

Keep It Moving

These rhymes are meant to keep
a line of jumpers moving through
the rope. One jumper runs in,
skips, then runs out while the next in
line takes a turn. These rhymes also
work for two jumpers at a time.

California oranges,
Fifty cents a pack,
Come on, *(name)*,
And tap me on the back.

*A second skipper enters the rope when named and
taps the original skipper on the back. The original
skipper jumps out and the rhyme begins again.*

Anna Banana had no sense,
She bought a piano for fifty cents.
But the only tune that she could play
Was "*(Skipper's name)*, get out of
    the donkey's way!"

*Skipper jumps out, when named, to avoid a kick from
the "donkey"—a new skipper.*

Keep the line moving so everyone gets a chance.

Down the Mississippi
Where the boats go push.

At "push," a new skipper jumps in and pushes out previous skipper.

Cross the Bible Belt
One by one,
Two by two . . .

This is a good rhyme for times you have one rope and lots of jumpers all clamoring for a turn. The skippers form lines of equal numbers on either side of rope. At "one by one," one skipper from each side runs in, jumps once and exits on the opposite side. At "two by two," two from each side repeat the action, and so on. Decide beforehand who will come in at each number.

Down in the kitchen,
Doin' a bit of stichin,"
In comes a burglar
And knocks you out.

*At "in," a second skipper jumps in. At "out," the first
jumper is shoved out by the second.*

Count to ten with closed eyes.
A-baby one, a-baby two
A-baby three, four, five.
Baby, I don't take no little jive.
A-baby six, a-baby seven
A-baby eight, nine, ten.
You better back it up and do it again.

On a mountain stands a lady.
Who she is, I do not know.
All she wants is gold and silver,
All she wants is Big Fat Joe.
So jump in, *(new skipper's name)*,
And jump out, *(original skipper's name)*.
On a mountain stands a lady . . .

*Skipper jumps until joined by another, then jumps
out when told.*

Kings and Queens and partners two,
Here are the things that you must do:
Stand at ease.
Bend your knees.
Salute to the east.
Bow to the west.
Shake it to the one
That you like best.

Skippers perform the actions described, ending with a
wiggly dance step at "shake it." Or the skippers can
run out and tag a new pair of skippers.

My mother and your mother live
    across the way.
Every night they have a fight and
    this is what they say:

Acka wacka
Soda cracker,
Acka wacka boo.
Acka wacka
Soda cracker,
Out goes you!

"Bend your knees."

189

"Acka, wacka soda cracker . . ."

Every morning at eight o'clock,
You can hear the postman knock.
One, two, three, four,
There goes *(name)* out the door.

*Skipper jumps out on the last line and is replaced by
a new skipper. If jumping loners, skipper may click
handles for each knock instead.*

House to let,
Inquire within.
When *(name)* moves out
Let *(second name)* jump in.

*New skipper replaces the previous one each time
the verse is repeated.*

Polly put the kettle on
And have a cup of tea.
In comes *(name)*
And out goes me!

*New skipper comes in and original skipper exits
the rope on the last line.*

Pom, pom pompadour,
(Skipper's name) is calling
(Second name) to the door.
(Second skipper)'s the one
Who's going to have some fun,
So we don't need *(first skipper)* any more.

*Continue chanting, calling in new skippers and
sending the old ones out.*

Queen bee chasing me,
I call in *(name)*.

(Skipper's name) is in love with *(boy'name)*,
He's her only man.
(Skipper's name) is in love with *(boy'name)*,
Catch her if you can.

*All players chase the skipper through the rope,
around an ender and back through the rope, over
and over until the skipper is tagged.*

Two little sausages frying in a pan,
One went POP and the other went BANG!

*Two skippers jump together until one hops out one
side of the rope at "pop," the other jumps out the
opposite side at "bang."*

"One went Pop and the other went Bang!"

Join In

These rhymes call in jumpers and keep them coming until there's hardly any room left to breathe, let alone jump.

"January, February, March . . ."
Sheep in the meadow, cow in the corn.
Jump in on the month that you were born.
January, February, March . . .

A, B, C, 1, 2, 3,
I want *(name)* to come in with me.

Second skipper joins the first in the rope when named, then the second skipper chants the rhyme, inviting in a third, and so on until the rope is full.

Everyone seems to know this one:

All in together, girls.
How is the weather, girls?
When is your birthday?
Please jump in.
January, February, March . . .
(Continue through the calendar. Each skipper jumps
in when her birthday month is called. Once all
skippers are in the rope, the next rhyme is sung.)
When is your birthday?
Please jump out.
January, February, March . . .

All in together, very fine weather.
I see teacher looking out the wind-er.
Ding dong, fire drill! Ding, dong, fire drill!
January, February, March . . .

*Skippers jump through all twelve months. This rhyme
is more fun the more jumpers you squeeze into the
rope, all trying to jump together.*

Changing bedrooms number one.
Changing bedrooms number two.
Changing bedrooms number three . . . .

*An equal number of skippers stands on each side of
the rope. With each verse, one or all run through the
rope, exchanging sides with the opposite jumper.*

Crossing the bridge to London Town,
One jumps up and the other down.

*One skipper stands while the other crouches, touching
the ground. Skippers switch actions on the next jump.*

Our boots are made of leather,
Our stockings are made of silk,
Our slips are made of cotton
As white as white as milk.
Here we go around, around,
And then we all must touch the ground.

Skippers spin and touch the ground when told.

"sunny, sunny weather."

Rainy, rainy weather, all go out together.
January, February, March . . .

Skippers all exit at December.

Some love coffee, some love tea.
I want *(name)* to come in with me.

*Skipper named jumps in, then recites the rhyme
naming another new jumper. This continues until
the rope is full or until someone misses.*

Sunny, sunny weather,
All come in together.
January, February, March . . .

Skippers enter on their birthday months.

Sloooow Salt and
RED HOT PEPPER!

If jumpers know only one skipping game it's probably pepper. That's because it's hot hot hot! It can be played by a loner or with a group.

Whenever a rhyme uses the word "pepper"—or variations of it like "hot," "red hot," and "red hot peppers"—the enders begin to turn the rope faster and faster until the skipper can't keep up. The association with pepper was made because this move really turns up the heat. Sometimes other words are used, though, so look for words in italics. That's your cue to move!

Whenever a rhyme mentions salt, the rope is turned oh-so-slowly, just enough to keep it moving.

Because these rhymes are based on the use of the words salt and pepper, they're homey rhymes set mostly in the kitchen or grocery store. The many, many versions differ from each other by only a word or two.

Baker, baker,
Bake your bread
With salt, vinegar, mustard and *pepper!*

Buster Brown went to town
With his pants on upside down.
He lost a nickel,
He bought a pickle.
The pickle was sour,
he bought a flower.
The flower was yellow,
He met a fellow.
The fellow was mean,
He bought a bean.
The bean was hard,
He bought a card.
And on the card
It said, *"Red hot pepper!"*

Have a cherry, have a plum,
Have a piece of chewing gum,
Along with *red hot pepper!*

Mabel, Mabel,
set the table
and don't forget the *red hot pepper!*

"RED HOT PEPPER!"

A slightly longer version adds a series of slow turns at "salt" and goes:

Mabel, Mabel,
Set the table.
Don't forget the salt
And *pepper*!

I told Ma,
And Ma told Pa,
To give me some *red hot peas*.

If you're able, set the table,
Don't forget the salt.
If you're able, set the table,
Don't forget the *pepper*.

Alternate salts and peppers a set number of times or until the skipper misses.

Mother sent me to the store.
This is what she sent me for:
To get some coffee, tea and *pepper*.

Mother, Mother, I am able
To stand on a chair and set the table.
Daughter, daughter, don't forget
Salt, vinegar and *red hot pepper.*

Motorboat, motorboat, go so slow.
Motorboat, Motorboat, start to go.
Motorboat, motorboat, go so fast.
Motorboat, motorboat, step on the *gas*.

One for the money,
Two for the show,
Three to get ready,
And four to *go*!

One to make ready and two to prepare,
Luck to the rider and off goes the mare,
Salt, mustard, vinegar, *pepper.*

Pepsi Cola hits the spot
Turn the rope and give her hot.
H-O-T spells *hot.*

CHAPTER 9

Count Me Out:

Rhymes for Choosing Enders

Who gets to jump first? Who is stuck as an ender? Choosing enders and jumpers are important issues and the only fair way to settle them is with a rhyme.

Out goes Y-O-U!

Use the following rhymes to decide who's who. Then you can use them as running-out rhymes—the skipper jumps out when the last word is said.

A, B, C, D, E, F, G,
H, I, J, K, L, M, N, O, P,
Q, R, S, T, U are out!

Acka wacka soda cracka
Acka wacka boo.
If your father chews tabacca,
Out goes you.

As I was walking by the lake,
I saw a little rattlesnake.
I gave him so much jellycake,
It make his little belly ache.
1, 2, 3, out goes he *(or she)*.

Bake a pudding,
Bake a pie.
Did you ever tell a lie?
Yes, you did.
I know you did.
You broke your mama's teapot lid.
O-U-T spells out.

And out you must go,
Right in the middle
Of the deep blue sea.

Cinderella at a ball,
Cinderella had a fall.
When she fell, she lost her shoe.
Cinderella, Y-O-U.

Eeny meeny miney mo,
Catch a tiger by the toe.
If he hollers, let him go.
Eeny meeny miney mo.
Out goes you!

Fireman, fireman, number eight,
Hit his head against the gate.
The gate flew in, the gate flew out.
That's the way he put the fire out.
O-U-T spells out and out you go.

Ickle, ockle, bottle,
Ickle, ockle, out.
If you come to my house,
I will kick you out.
O-U-T spells out,
And out you go for saying so.

Inky, pinky, penny winky
Out goes she *(or he)*

Look up, sky blue,
All out but you.

Mickey Mouse bought a house.
Couldn't pay the rent and got kicked out.

Oh, dear me,
Momma caught a flea.
Flea died, Momma cried,
One, two, three.

One potato, two potato,
Three potato, four.
Five potato, six potato,
Seven potato, more.
One, two, three,
Out goes she *(or he)*.

One, two, three, four, five,
I caught a fish alive.
Six, seven, eight, nine, ten,
I let him go again.

One, two, three,
Tommy hurt his knee.
He couldn't slide,
And so he cried.
Out goes he *(or she)*.

Enders Rhymes

Here are some rhymes for *enders* to chant. They come in handy when your jumping partners are real pros.

Close your eyes and count to ten.
If you miss, you take an end.

If skipper is successful, add other challenges:
one-foot jump, spin, split.

Tomorrow, tomorrow, tomorrow
Never comes.
Tomorrow, tomorrow, tomorrow
Always runs.

Skipper runs out, or does a
running step on the last line.

In, spin,
Let *(name)*
come in.
Out, spout,
Let *(name)* go out.

The enders chant the
rhyme over and over,
naming a different jumper each time,
who must be ready to jump in or out when named.

"Come on in."

(Ender's name, ender's name) lived in a tent.
(Ender's name, ender's name) couldn't pay rent.
She borrowed one,
She borrowed two,
She passed the end along to you.

This is a handy rhyme to remember when someone's been stuck as an ender a little too long!

Everybody, everybody,
Come on in.
First one who misses
Must take my end.

If the enders want to be sure they don't have long to wait, they can turn the rope at pepper speed.

Five, ten, fifteen, twenty,
Nobody leaves the rope empty.
If they do, they shall suffer.
Take an end and be a duffer.

Skippers line up for a run at the rope. Each jumps in, skips once, then runs out and circles around to get back in line. Next time around, each jumps twice, then three times and so on, until someone misses and becomes an ender. The ender takes a place in line and the rhyme begins again.

Hey, *(name)*, somebody's calling your name!
Hey, *(name)*, somebody's playing your game!
(Skipper named jumps in and chants the rest of the rhyme)
I went downtown to listen to the clock.
It went tick tock tick tock, one o'clock.
Tick tock, tick tock, two o'clock.
Tick tock, tick tock, three o'clock . . .

This rhyme is begun by an ender, who gets to choose who the two jumpers will be. The skipper jumps up to twelve o'clock; enders may turn the rope at pepper speed.

"Please take an end."

Who stole the cookies from the cookie jar?
(Name) stole the cookies from the cookie jar!
(Skipper jumps in)
Who, me? Yes, you!
Couldn't be! Then who?
Who stole the cookies from the cookie jar?
(New name) stole the cookies from the
cookie jar!
"Who, me? . . .

*An ender begins this rhyme, chanting the first two
lines and choosing the first suspect in the crime. That
skipper jumps out after fingering another culprit, and
with the second skipper the pattern starts again.*

Here's a good-luck chant for
skippers who miss too often and are
always winding up as an ender:

Touch wood, no good.
Touch iron, rely on.

If that doesn't work, try this:

Leave the rope,
Stop the rope,
Please take an end.

CHAPTER 10

Fun and Games

What? Just jumping rope isn't enough for you? You want to do more? Well, luckily there are dozens of jump rope games you can play. Some require some funky jumping, but others don't use any jumping at all. They're arranged here in order of the numbers of players needed, from games for two to some that are best with lot of jumpers.

Some of these games are very old, dating back to ancient times.

Of course, feel free to adapt and change the rules to suit your situation and the number of players. We know you'll do it anyway.

Double Trouble:
Two in One Rope

These are called turning games, because the challenge is as much in the rope handling as in the jumping—sort of double whammy. The good news is that there are no winners and losers!

Two in one rope takes extra work.

Spoons In Spoons, two players jump in one rope, both facing forward. The rope is turned by the jumper in the back. That jumper swings the rope over both heads and the two skip together. Announce new moves, like the Jumping Jack, in advance so your partner knows what's coming up.

Spoons is a game for two good friends.

Kissing Cousins This game is like Spoons, except the two jumpers face each other. The skipper turning the rope has the advantage here because she knows where the rope is at all times. The other skipper has to jump almost by instinct—gauging when the rope is about to pass underfoot. Of course a loud "jump!" cue from his partner would help.

Watch those knees! Make small jumps to avoid banging into each other.

Siamese Twins Two jumpers skip side by side. The skippers' outer hands hold the ropes. Because there are two enders, you must coordinate the turning motion so you're working smoothly together. You're skipping at the same time as you turn, so there's a lot of coordinated togetherness going on here.

Try some fancy steps, with each of you making the reverse move, like mirror images of each other.

With two jumpers swinging the same rope, you'll need to concentrate on coordinating moves.

Eggbeater It takes some practice to get the Eggbeater just right.

Practice this way first: Both skippers turn their ropes side by side, facing the same direction. When your partner's rope is arching overhead, your rope is passing under your feet. The ropes are in opposite positions as you turn.

Once you get the up/down rhythm set and aren't distracted by what your partner does, try the true Eggbeater: Turn toward each other a bit, so that if the ropes weren't alternating patterns, they would touch. The ropes should just miss each other as they come around.

The eggbeater is a masterpiece of timing.

Just Visiting One player turns the rope loners at first. Then the second jumper runs in and the two jump together for a while before the second jumper exits again.

In other versions of this game, two jumpers can enter together, or several jumpers can enter one at a time. Just remember to let out more rope each time. The longer the rope, the more jumpers you can have over for "Strawberry Shortcake."

The skipper turning the rope must widen the turn as soon as the other jumper enters.

220

Two's Company
Games for Three or More

Three may be a crowd, but it's just the number you need for these. While they can be played with many more jumpers, three is the minimum you need to keep the games going.

The more the merrier.

The Clock There are several games with this or a similar name. For some reason the clock has powerful jump rope connections. Maybe because jumping rope is all in the timing!

During this game, a skipper performs the listed motions, while the enders chant the hours:

One o'clock (*run in, jump once, run out*)
Two o'clock (*run in, jump twice, run out*)
Three o'clock (*jump three times*)
Four o'clock (*jump four times*)
Five o'clock (*jump five times*)
Six o'clock (*high waters*)
Seven o'clock (*low waters*)
Eight o'clock (*hop eight times*)
(no blancing hop, stay in rope)
Nine o'clock (*hop on one foot with
    one eye closed*)
Ten o'clock (*jump ten times with
    both eyes closed*)
Eleven o'clock (*jump eleven times with
    feet crossed*)
Twelve o'clock (*cross feet while jumping
    twelve times*)

High Low This game begins with the chant:

Charlie over the water,
Charlie over the sea,
Charlie caught a blackbird,
But he can't catch me!

After "me," the enders raise the rope and turn it over the skipper's head while the skipper crouches. The rhyme is chanted again. This time, after "me" they lower the rope to turn normally while the skipper stands and jumps. The timing is harder than it sounds!

The timing is harder than it sounds!

High, Low, Dolly, Pepper This is a game of alternating steps. The enders turn the rope, calling out High, Low, Dolly, or Pepper.

The enders give the skipper one jump's warning that they'll be changing turning style. On "High", they raise the rope off the ground, on

"Low" return it to the ground. "Dolly" forces the skipper to perform a fancy step and "Pepper" means . . . well, you know what *that* means!

Enders warn the skipper about which step to use.

Jump-the-Shot For this game, tie a sneaker to one end of the rope. An ender stands in between two players or inside a circle of them. Each jumper is just within range of the rope. The ender spins the rope in a circle, close to the ground at first, then higher and higher— and faster and faster. The players all jump the rope as the sneaker whips under them. As the rope spins, players may chant:

Anyone who gets his feet snagged by the rope is out.

Angel, Devil, Angel, Devil . . .

Each player is doomed to be whatever she misses on.

Rhymes In this game an ender thinks of the first line of a rhyme involving the skipper's name. For example:

Susan, Susan, stayed up late

Then the skipper has four jumps to think up a rhyme. No fair starting with "orange"!

Rocking the Boat The enders swing the rope back and forth as the skipper bounces a ball or spins in the air during each jump.

In this game, a jumper uses a ball to make Bluebell jumps more interesting.

Rock the Baby

This is a simple game that's a high-jumping challenge. Enders swing the rope back and forth without an overhand turn. Skippers jump twice, then run out. Raise the rope for the next turn, higher and higher, until someone misses.

Enders keep raising the rope higher and higher until someone misses.

Serpents or Over the Waves

In Serpents, the rope is whipped back and forth on the ground to make wide S-shaped curves. In Over the Waves, the rope is whipped up and down, creating waves. In both versions, the aim is for a jumper to leap over the rope without touching it. In Over the Waves, the enders might chant:

Jump over the ocean,
Jump over the sea.

This game makes it fun to be an ender!

Baking Bread The first skipper jumps into the rope carrying a ball, stone, small stuffed toy, or other object. The skipper drops it and exits the rope. The enders should raise the rope, if needed, to make room for the object. The next skipper must pick up the object and jump with it at least once. Then that skipper drops it and is replaced by another skipper.

You'll need a prop for baking bread.

Begging This one is just plain silly. Two skippers enter the rope side by side. One skipper chants:

Give me some bread and butter.

The other replies

I haven't any; try next door.

Then the skippers switch positions while jumping. The two resume the rhyme and continue to switch positions until one misses. Then the skippers switch places with the enders.

In Begging, one skipper crosses in front of the other inside the rope.

Chase the Fox Foxes show up quite a bit in jump rope games. In this one, the fox, or leader, runs through the rope followed by all the other players, each timing their run so that the rope isn't touched. Once everyone is through, the fox runs back in the other direction, once again followed by the others.

Skippers can't touch the rope when playing chase the fox.

The third time through the rope, the fox jumps once, the next time twice, and so on, each time followed by the others who all do the name number of skips. Anyone who misses is replaced by an ender, who takes up where the other left off.

Colors In this game, each ender chooses a color, keeping it a secret. The other players run through the rope, one after the other, yelling a color. If a jumper guesses the enders' color, the jumper must take the ender's place. If not, the jumper runs through again with a second guess.

Try naming food items in a grocery store or sweets in a candy shop. Then again, anything goes!

Guessing a secret is always fun, but it's even more so when it means someone stops being an ender!

Do As the Old Fox in Front of You

Begin with a line of players. The first jumps in and chooses a step, then all follow doing the same step. The second time around, the second jumper becomes the leader, choosing a new jump that every one must copy in turn. Each jumper has a shot at the fox. (That's *being* the fox, of course, not shooting the fox.)

This funny name comes from Italy, where this version of Follow the Leader is played.

Tag You can probably guess how this one is played: A skipper jumps in while a rhyme is chanted challenging the other players to a game of tag. The players chase the skipper into the rope, out, and around one of the enders. Then it's back into the rope and around again and again, until the skipper is tagged. Whoever is caught is an ender.

The skipper can name a player, or all players can take up the chase.

Up and Down Two enders stand sideways, both facing in the same direction. Each holds the end of a long rope. One ender starts turning. The second ender begins to turn just as the other ender's side of the rope is arching overhead.

This turning game has a snaky movement.

When an up-and-down rhythm gets going, one ender's half of the rope is smacking the ground when the other's half is arching at its peak.

Two jumpers then enter the rope, one after the other, one on each end. Once you've gotten jumping aced, try touching the ground on your balancing hop. This will create a cool, machine like up-and-down motion.

High Water, Low Water No surprises here! The name pretty much says it all. The rope is held taut by the enders. They raise it to various heights for skippers to jump over or lower it for them to wriggle or back-bend under, as in playing Limbo.

As they raise the rope, the enders can chant:

When it rains, the Mississippi River
Gets higher and higher and higher . . .

Chinese Rope Kicking Two enders hold the rope straight, about a foot off the ground. Each player takes a running start at the rope, but instead of jumping over it, gives it a kick. If you miss, it's an end for you. This is not as easy as it sounds, because the rope is a very thin target.

After everyone has had a shot at that height, the rope is moved up and everyone goes again.

It's not easy as it seems to kick the rope.

Scambled Eggs This game is about cramming as many people into the rope as possible.

Two enders turn a long rope while one skipper chants:

Get out the pan,
Get out the butter,
Get out the eggs and put them in the pan.
One, two, three . . .

At each number called, another skipper runs in and skips along with the others. When no more jumpers can fit, the first skipper yells, "Scrambled Eggs," and the enders turn at pepper speed. You'll see why you yell "scrambled eggs." When everyone tries skipping together at high speeds, things can get messy.

There's something really funny about jumping to a silly rhyme with lots of friends. You may miss simply because you're laughing so hard.

Keep the Kettle Boiling In this game, a line of skippers runs through the rope, one after another, when named. The two enders may chant:

Keep the kettle boiling just for *(name)*.
One, two, and a dibble-dabble three.

Steps Just when you thought the rope couldn't get any higher . . .

For this one, you need at least two ropes and two sets of enders. The enders position their ropes one beside the other and turn at various heights off the ground, creating a series of steps. The first pair may be turning Bluebells. Skippers must jump through each rope in turn, first once, then twice and so on.

Over the Rainbow This looks great when it's done well. You'll need at least five people and three ropes of various lengths. Two enders turn the longest rope. They use their whole arms to make the arch as high as possible. Inside that rope, two more enders jump, turning a slightly shorter rope. They face in the same direction. And inside both of these ropes, a jumper skips loners with her own rope.

Three ropes pass overhead at the same time, but at different heights, creating a rainbow effect.

The Umbrella

This game is best done with at least three ropes, each with two enders. The enders are arranged in a circle, as if they were numbers on a clock, with pairs of enders facing each other across the circle, resting their ropes on the ground. They chant this rhyme to begin the game:

A, B, C,
Count of three,
1, 2, 3, go ! "

The umbrella calls for some amazing cooperation.

A skipper jumps in the middle of the umbrella.

At "go," all pairs of enders begin turning at once, all in the same counter-clockwise direction. When all the ropes are turning smoothly, a skipper runs through, making sure not to touch any of the ropes.

Another way to play is by having the skipper in the middle taking one skip toward each "hour" of the clock.

Double Dutch If jump rope is fun, Double Dutch is twice the fun. It's also twice as hard, so wait until you've really gotten the hang of single jumping before trying this game.

With a name like Double Dutch, it shouldn't come as a surprise to learn that you need two ropes. Each should be at

A Double Dutch turner needs a lot of practice.

least 12 feet long. Some stores sell jump ropes especially for Double

Dutch, or you can make one yourself.

Even though there are two ropes, there are still just two enders. The ropes alternate positions, swinging just inches from each other as they turn, just like the beaters on a mixer. That takes a lot of practice. A lot.

Time the turns so that one rope smacks the ground just as the other reaches its peak. Your left hand will be moving clockwise and your right counterclockwise.

If you think things are tough for the enders, just remember this: Two ropes mean twice as many jumps. So many jumps, and so quickly, that most Double Dutch jumpers use alternate feet. You'll look like you're running in place when the ropes really get going.

It's hard running in, too. Double Dutch jumpers sneak in between ropes by running in from behind an ender. Then it's Up the Ladder to the center of the ropes. Don't try to run into the ropes at the center, as you do in Into the Wall—it really will be like slamming into a wall. Running out takes perfect timing, too. Leave the ropes the way you came in, by running past an ender.

Many Double Dutch players are too breathless from jumping or turn-

"My mother, your mother, yap, yap, yap."

ing to chant rhymes. Some just count in different ways. But when they do use rhymes, counting rhymes are popular. One jumper exits just as the next runs in, creating a tricky moment when they almost meet in the ropes.

Here are some rhymes sung especially for Double Dutch:

One rope is on the bottom,
The other's on the top.
When I say "hot," go faster,
When I say "miss," you stop.
Hot! . . . Miss!

The skipper jumps at pepper speed as long as possible, then deliberately stops the rope at "miss."

My mother, your mother, yap, yap, yap.
They chatter on the phone
And never seem to stop.
They stay at home all day
And never, ever visit,
When someone rings the doorbell,
I just yell,"Who is it?"

Another player yells out her name and enters the rope as the first jumper exits.

Girls, girls, do you want to fight?
Here comes *(friend's name)*
With her pants on tight.
Second jumper joins the first in the rope.
She can wiggle,
She can woggle,
She can do all that,
I bet you ten dollars that she can't do this:
Count to ten with closed eyes.

*Original jumper counts while second jumper begins
jumping with eyes closed.*

A-baby one,
A-baby two,
A-baby three, four, five.
Baby, I don't take no little jive.
A-baby six,
A-baby seven,
A-baby eight, nine, ten.
You better back it up and do it again.

My landlord rings my front doorbell,
A ding dong chime.
Lets it ring for a good long time.
Peek through the windows,
Peek through the blinds,
Ask the man what he got on his mind.
Says, "A-money, honey."
One, two
Says, "A-money, honey."
Three, four,
Says, "A-money, honey,
Or I throw you out!"

Skipper jumps out.

I left my wife and 22 kids alone all night
Without any bread.
Did I do right? No, I left.
I left my wife and 22 kids alone in the house
Without any bread.
Left? Right!
I left my wife and 22 kids alone all night
Without any bread . . .

*This rhyme takes advantage of the alternate-foot
rhythm used in Double Dutch. Time your jumps so you
land on your left foot every time you say "left," and
your right foot every time you say "right."*

Chinese Jump Rope Chinese Jump Rope became a craze in the United States in the 1960s, and it's still popular here today. You can buy Chinese Jump Rope elastics, but just as often jumpers use a standard jump rope knotted to form a circle.

Instead of holding the rope, the two enders stand with it looped around their legs. They stand with legs apart to create a rectangular skipping area. First the rope is looped at ankle height, then at the knees. Raise it higher, if you dare!

This game is called Tio pi Jin in China.

Skippers hop in, out and over the rectangle in different combinations, some of them going on and on. In some steps, you catch the rope with your feet deliberately, creating patterns in the rope.

Here are some basic steps.

In

In Hop into the center with both feet.

Out Leave the rope with a leap and land on both feet.

On

Over Jump clean over the rectangle and land with both feet outside the rope on the opposite side.

On Touching the rope by mistake is taboo, but in this move you touch it on purpose. Jump and land with a foot on both sides of the rope. The rope is now grounded.

251

Straddle   Jump up and spread your legs apart as you drop. When you land, your body is over the rectangle, but your legs are straddling the outside of the ropes.

Straddle

Hook   This is not a jump but a sliding move. Stand beside the jumping area. Scoop up the rope with the nearest foot and take a big step. One side of the rope is now stretched over in a point that crosses the other side. Tap your toe and then step back to restorethe rope to its original position.

Hook

Side-by-Side A quick-quick-quick series of three jumps. First jump up and land with only one foot in the rope. Without pausing, jump again, shifting sideways so that the foot that was in is now out on the other side and the foot that was out is now in. Then shift again so that both feet are out on the opposite side from the one you entered.

Side-by-Side

Diamond This isn't a jump, it's a starting position. Facing an ender, hook the rope with the outside of your foot (a tricky move) and jump two-footed over the other side, bringing the first rope over with you. Then spread your legs wide so that the two crossed ropes form a diamond shape.

Here are some combinations
to play in Chinese Jump Rope.
Two have rhymes and are called
"ordinaries" and "opposites."

Ordinaries: Tinker, tinker, Over, Out

Skipper jumps in on the second "tinker," then jumps out.

Opposites: Tinker, Over, Tinker, In, Out.

Skipper does nothing on the first "tinker," but on "over"
leaps a side-by-side. Then the skipper leaps in and out.

This rhyme asks you to jump In, do
a Criss-Cross move and jump Out,
then in again for a Kick, then Out.
Then you jump an Over and finally
do a Split over both sides.

I can do the criss-cross,
I can do the kick,
I can do the overall,
And also the split.

Other rhymes, simply chant the names of the moves being jumped. They may be called out by the jumper or the enders. The jumper follows the directions as quickly as possible. A typical combination could include any pattern of steps, like this one:

Out, In, Straddle, Side by Side, On, In, Out.

Skip the Skip: Rope Games That Don't Use Jumping

Toes tired? Looking for a game that won't make you leap? Here are some that use your jump rope but are hop free.

Caught in the Net In Africa, children play this tag game using a rope. It's called "A-Fishing." Players are divided into fishermen and fish. An area is blocked off with two "safe" areas on either side—the "banks" of the river. The fish wander around inside the play area until the fishermen arrive. These players are spaced out along the rope. As they enter, they chant

We come, we come, we come, we come,
We are fishermen.
We come out a-fishing, oh!
We come a-fishing, oh!
Haul the fish in, catch them, so!

The fishermen try to capture fish in their net by circling unwary players with the rope. The fish can run into the safe areas to avoid being caught but can stay only a set period of time, counting out the seconds as they wait. As fish are caught, they join the fishermen on the net.

"Fish" run to avoid being caught in the net.

Tug of War Who *hasn't* played this one? Kids have played it since the days of ancient Greece and probably before that. It's been a big hit ever since. Here's the classic way to play.

Divide players into two teams. To make the game challenging, try to make the teams as evenly matched in terms of weight and strength as possible. Draw a line on the ground, or better yet scrape it into the dirt—players may end up falling on their butts, so grass is a better surface than concrete for this one.

Stretch the rope across the line, with members of each side spaced out along the rope. A smart team puts its heaviest player at the end. That player is the anchor. At the shout of "1, 2, 3, go!" each side heaves and tugs in an attempt to drag the other team over the line.

Tug of War II Push, pull . . . you choose! If tugging isn't your game, try this version of the old favorite. Draw a line, as before. Each team lines up along the line, facing each other. The rope is held along and over the line, instead of across it. Each player holds onto the rope with both hands. At the signal, everyone pushes.

Set a time limit. When time's up, count the number of players who have managed to push their way over the line. The team with the most who have crossed is the winner.

*Everyone knows how to play
Tug of War.*

That's the end of the book, but you've probably been dreaming up more rhymes and games just by switching around some of the rules. Write yours down; maybe they'll make it into a book one day!

And most of all have fun skipping!

Rhymes Index

This is a listing of the first lines of the rhymes in this book. Rhymes that begin with a name or word you fill in are listed together at the end of this index. Remember, you can also look up rhymes by their categories. Check in the Table of Contents for the category page numbers.

Games, Jumps and Jargon Index

Special thanks to all the skippers that helped make
this book possible:

The Kangaroo Kids of Columbia Maryland coached
by Jean Hodges and Jim McCleary: Jim, Carissa,
Marie, Paige, Amanda, Melissa, Ashley, Marissa,
Jessica E., Jessica D., Katherine, Elizabeth, Jasmine,
Timothy and Emily.

Sophie, Clayton,
Lakisha, Demetria,
Julian, Missy Kenneth,
Shaneka, Kenisha,
Kellen, Marni and
Hanako.

Jennifer Armstrong and her after-school kids at Hartley House, New York, NY: Terri, Sean, Yvette, Kyndell, Tay, Jadira, Emily, Tina and Hanako.

The Louis Morris Gazelles Double Dutch Team of the Bronx: Alfredo, Natasha, Michael, Sylvia, China, India, Taisha, Delilah, Christina, Venus, April, Nixaviera, Jose, Patricia, Shanita, Caridad, Erica, Victoria, Joanna, Jeannie and Jessica.

Special thanks to the dozens of kids who shared their favorite skipping verses. Thanks to the people on America Online who filled my virtual mail-box—especially: Maggi, Taisha, Ron, Kelly, Lisa, Matt, Michael, Wendy, Amber, Corey, Jan, the Eckel family, Devin, Rose, Crystal, Helen, Becky, Eric, Kenny, Susan, Bryan, and the Chan family.

The fifth graders in Mrs. Loredo's class at the St. Francis School in Metuchen, NJ.

The kids of the New York Volunteer Services for Children program—especially: Natasha, Jessica, Vanessa and Jessica and Sandra Hidalgo.

And a special thank you goes to my family and friends for allowing me to interrupt weddings, dinners, and parties with my notebook—especially Stephanie and Stacey for their Canadian perspective.